Developing Mul

The personal side of creative expression

Copyright © 2011 by Douglas Eby

Talent Development Resources
talentdevelop.com

Ø Ø Ø

Praises :

"Part book about creativity, part compendium of useful tidbits, quotations and research results, and part annotated bibliography, this is a wildly useful and highly entertaining resource. Douglas Eby, a multi-talented writer himself, provides intriguing tastes of amazingly varied and comprehensive views of creativity, creators and the creative life, plus where and how to find more."

– Stephanie S. Tolan, fiction writer and consultant on the needs of the gifted; co-author of the book Guiding the Gifted Child.
www.stephanietolan.com
www.storyhealer.com

~ ~ ~

"Packed full of insights and resources for the creative life, Developing Multiple Talents offers new ways to thrive as a creative person. Douglas Eby addresses many of the issues we face - fear, lack of confidence and focus - allowing the creative person to feel understood and ultimately empowered. Normalizing the challenges in the creative process provides a huge step toward coping with those challenges. Douglas's book gives readers a resource for understanding and accepting our problems and our gifts. I highly recommend Developing Multiple Talents as a resource for anyone who wants to understand the psychology behind our creative drive."

– Cynthia Morris, Writing and creativity coach.
Site: Original Impulse
www.originalimpulse.com

~ ~ ~

"In my practice working with gifted and talented individuals, I have consistently encountered characteristics, psychological processes and temperaments that commonly overlap. Other books have focused on these aspects individually, but Douglas Eby does an extraordinary job of integrating these complex and dimensional characteristics into a complete overview of the multitalented personality. Developing Multiple Talents is pivotal in providing a thorough understanding and a more comprehensive portrait of the gifted, creative and talented individual. Eby's extensive collection of previous research, writings and interviews will reshape how we perceive and view the artist, actor or inventor."

– Lisa A. Riley, MA, LMFT, Creativity coach and Licensed Marriage & Family Therapist, The Art of Mind theartofmind.com Therapy4Artists.com

~ ~ ~

"It is not always easy to host a kind of overdose of talents: Often one career direction is not a sufficient outlet for one's creative thrusts. And being basically uncommon may impede the finding of proper peers as a guide or reference for personal maturation. Douglas Eby's book is kaleidoscopical, just like the subject he describes. Every turn of a page offers new and colorful peers that reflect on the book's ingredients. The many links make it possible to read in different levels of detail. The chapters help the reader not to get overwhelmed, that is, if you know when to pause reading."

– Willem Kuipers, counselor on career and development of identity for extra intelligent people; author of the book Enjoying the Gift of Being Uncommon: Extra Intelligent, Intense, and Effective.
Site: www.ximension.com

~ ~ ~ ~ ~

Appreciation

My grateful thanks to everyone who has so generously provided such helpful and encouraging feedback and reviews - and more thanks to all those who do so much research and writing in the area of creativity and personal growth.

Douglas Eby

Ø Ø Ø

Introduction

*"I want to do wardrobe. I want to do hair. I want to do makeup...
writing...directing...producing.
I want to do all of it. I like it."*
Abigail Breslin

Many people share an enthusiasm for exploring and expressing multiple creative talents and passions. The dynamic complexity of creative abilities in multitalented people is a huge field of study. I have been researching and writing on aspects of creativity and high ability for more than twenty years, and almost daily find some new and intriguing perspectives from research studies, blogs, artist interviews and other sources.

My hope is that you find material in this brief overview book to be of interest and value in pointing toward areas to more deeply explore, to help you more fully realize your own abilities.

The cover image - <u>Digital Color Wheel</u> by Frank Bonilla (used under a Creative Commons license) - reminds me of the complexity and interaction of creative talents, and also of stained glass Rose windows in Gothic Cathedrals, which I find powerful and visually exciting.

My series of websites, columns and articles - and now this book - have grown out of my graduate studies in psychology, and personal research of more than twenty years to better understand my own social, emotional, personal development and achievement challenges, and to publish material that might help other people as well.

The kinds of questions I was exploring when I began my main site Talent Development Resources more than ten years ago continue to interest and challenge me, and of course many other people - topics like:

Why did I feel and think so differently from mainstream culture?

Why haven't I ever "settled down" into a specific career?

Why am I so sensitive to outer sensations and my own inner world?

Why have I been so self-critical?

What makes me and so many creative people vulnerable to dark moods like depression and anxiety at times?

How can I increase my satisfaction and emotional reward from what I am doing with my life?

What does research say about enhancing creative expression?

Do you relate to any of those?

There are many areas of psychology and other fields which I continue to explore related to those questions – such as, positive psychology and happiness research, high sensitivity, mood and creativity, creative motivation, being a creative and highly sensitive entrepreneur, self concept, personal achievement – and other topics, many of which are at least briefly covered in this book.

I have never had the sense of being on a career path. Barbara Sher writes about many people being "Scanners" (see the Work - Career chapter) - but I have had rich experiences in many interesting (and many not so interesting) jobs, including glue testing in a chemical company lab; collecting beach sand for a marine zoologist; growing bread mold at CalTech for a geneticist; working as an assistant for a psychiatrist doing some of the early left-right brain research; repairing woodwind instruments; operating computer-controlled visual effects motion picture cameras, and working as a psychology counselor with depressed or addicted people.

Along the way, I've also done some photography, and acting in community theater plays, and as a movie extra. I've also led support groups for gifted women.

"All creative people have multiple talents, don't they?"

In his post <u>Creatives With Multiple Talents</u> (on his blog <u>The Artist's Road</u>), Patrick Ross writes about meeting two students in a Masters in Writing program who are about to graduate, one of whom had performed on the violin and the other had acting experience and performed magic tricks.

Ross commented to them he thought it was interesting that all of these writing students had another talent they could perform, and writes that the violin player "looked at me as if I had just expressed bafflement that an orange was the color orange," and said "All creative people have multiple talents, don't they?"

Ross adds, "They do, scientists tell us, even if they don't realize it. After all, if you've never picked up a musical instrument, you may not realize you have a predisposition to excel at it. But the creative brain knows how to both master a skill and think in ways others would find counter-intuitive to breathe new life into that skill."

Examples of multitalented people

The opening quote by actor Abigail Breslin is a sample of many people who are creatively passionate and ambitious from childhood. The young actress has a number of movie credits including her endearing role in "Little Miss Sunshine." Now about age 14, she has time to pursue her varied interests, and I look forward to seeing more of her dynamic work. [The undated quote is from imdb.com - the Internet Movie Database - a great source of information on movie projects and people.]

Arts and entertainment fields attract many creatively multitalented people - perhaps especially filmmaking. A number of well-known actors, for example, create projects outside of acting. Creativity researcher James C. Kaufman, Ph.D. uses a term I like for people having such multiple passions and abilities: **creative polymathy**. See more about this in the last chapter.

Here are a few examples of well-known people that you may find interesting and even inspiring. But I also offer a warning: Just because we don't match some of these people in terms of achievement, doesn't mean we are not in fact multitalented. There are many issues and influences affecting how fully we can realize our abilities. That's one of the points of this book.

Julia Cameron is well-known as the author of The Artist's Way, and has been a writer since the age of eighteen, creating short stories, essays and political journalism articles, and more than thirty books including a crime novel plus volumes of children's poems and prayers. She is also an award-winning poet and playwright, with extensive film and theater credits, including writing an episode of the TV show Miami Vice, and writer and director of the movie God's Will. She collaborated with her former husband Martin Scorsese on three films. For her musicals, Cameron serves as composer as well as libretto-writer and lyricist.

She has a quote on her site www.theartistsway.com that I really appreciate: "Most of us have no idea of our real creative height. We are much more gifted than we know."

Jamie Lee Curtis has written a number of children's books. **Jane Seymour** is author of several books and art kits, and is an accomplished and widely published painter. **Bryce Dallas Howard** has credits as a vocalist for a movie soundtrack, for musical production, and as a producer, screenwriter and director.

Before graduating from Harvard with a psychology degree, **Natalie Portman** was credited as a research assistant to Alan Dershowitz and was co-author of a study on memory called "Frontal Lobe Activation During Object Permanence" that was published in a scientific journal.

James Franco was enrolled in Yale University's English PhD program, and has earned a master's degree from New York University's Tisch School of the Arts and Columbia University's MFA writing programs.

Jeff Bridges, 61, an Oscar winner for his acting, is releasing his first music album, a 10-song collection called "Jeff Bridges." He comments, "People like to put things in a box — and they do that with their own lives too, they limit things — but it's all art to me…all art is truth. People try to define things and make it easier for their mind to digest things, I guess. But music has been part of my life since I was a kid. Music meant more to me when I was young, but I went into acting because of family and because it was the path of least resistance." He added, "So many actors play music, and so many musicians want to act." [From "Jeff Bridges plays to his musician side," By Geoff Boucher, Los Angeles Times, August 15, 2011.]

Gordon Parks (1912-2006) was often referred to as a renaissance man, as noted in an obituary by Dennis McLellan [Los Angeles Times March 8, 2006], and lived up to the label: "In addition to his photography, film work and poetry, he composed a symphony, sonatas, concertos, film scores, and wrote novels, instructional photography manuals, essays and three memoirs. He received numerous honors over the years, including the National Medal of Arts from President Reagan. He was a high school dropout."

In my Creative Mind post Amber Benson on Writing: Creating is Kind of Intoxicating, I wrote about the actor (she played 'Tara' on "Buffy the Vampire Slayer") who also has multiple credits as a novelist and screenwriter, director and producer.

Another example is **Viggo Mortensen**, well-known for his acting in the The Lord of the Rings movies and many others, including Eastern Promises, and The Road. He portrays Sigmund Freud in the upcoming movie A Dangerous Method. In addition to acting, his creative pursuits include painting, photography, poetry, music, plus spoken-word recordings. In

2002, he founded Perceval Press to publish the works of his and other artists and authors.

He once commented: "Photography, painting or poetry - those are just extensions of me, how I perceive things, they are my way of communicating." (imdb.com)

He has made other comments that also relate to topics in this book, such as these: "If I don't get a little time by myself every day, it makes me uncomfortable. I really need that. Even if it's a minute or two. I think it was Robert Louis Stevenson who said this. It was about meandering through a career, or the arts in general, without seeming to have a deliberate plan. He said, 'To travel hopefully is better than to arrive, and the true success is in the labor.' That's a great line, 'To travel hopefully.' That's what I'd like to do. People who are creators create. People say to me all the time, 'Why don't you just focus on one thing?' And I say, 'Why? Why just one thing? Why can't I do more? Who makes up these rules?'" [From the site "Viggo Mortenson: Movies to Art to Politics" www.brego.net]

A profile says he "Speaks fluent English, Spanish, Danish, and French, but he also speaks Swedish and Norwegian reasonably well." [imdb.com]

Many highly creative people are uncommonly intelligent like that - though intellect and creativity are not the same ability, of course, nor do they always go with each other. But I will cover more about that below.

An Exploration

This is not designed as a how-to or self-help book, so much as an overview of some of the key aspects of our personality and inner life that can affect how well we understand, access and express our different creative talents - and be able to do much more than one thing. Along the way, though, there are suggestions by coaches, psychologists and others on strategies to help you explore more topics.

The chapters here are "headlines" about a variety of inter-related subjects, with brief summaries of topics, plus quotes by creative people and some excerpts from research studies, as well as links to additional resources.

Ø Ø Ø

Contents

Ø Ø Ø

> *Traits and Qualities*

INTELLIGENCE

One form of talent is obviously cognitive ability. How does that relate to other forms, such as creative ability? In the fields of writing and filmmaking, for example, there are many examples of prominent achievers who are highly intelligent, with or without academic credentials; but there are also many very creative and productive people without uncommon intellect.

Multiple Intelligences / Multiple Talents

Educator Howard Gardner of Harvard articulated his ideas of Multiple Intelligences in several books including Frames of Mind.
In his article Reframing the Mind, Daniel T. Willingham (a professor of psychology at the University of Virginia) noted a number of intelligence researchers have discussed various human abilities, including aesthetic,

athletic, musical, and so on, and "called them talents or abilities, whereas Gardner has renamed them intelligences."

He notes that Gardner thinks people possess at least eight independent types of intelligence, and provides this list of definitions, with examples Gardner has provided of professions that draw heavily on that particular intelligence:

• Linguistic: facility with verbal materials (writer, attorney).

• Logico-mathematical: the ability to use logical methods and to solve mathematical problems (mathematician, scientist).

• Spatial: the ability to use and manipulate space (sculptor, architect).

• Musical: the ability to create, perform, and appreciate music (performer, composer).

• Bodily-kinesthetic: the ability to use one's body (athlete, dancer).

• Interpersonal: the ability to understand others' needs, intentions, and motivations (salesperson, politician).

• Intrapersonal: the ability to understand one's own motivations and emotions (novelist, therapist with self-insight).

• Naturalist: the ability to recognize, identify, and classify flora and fauna or other classes of objects (naturalist, cook).

According to Prof. Willingham, "Gardner claims that everyone has all eight intelligences to some degree, but each individual has his or her own pattern of stronger and weaker intelligences. Gardner also argues that most tasks require more than one intelligence working together."

Isn't that true for multi-talented people in general?

A neurobiologist or actor may also have high levels of other talents or "intelligences" and make use of them in their profession - or not.

Maybe they paint or write short stories "on the side" and never publish, but they are still multi-talented.

Do we need a high IQ to be creative?

Creativity researcher Mihaly Csikszentmihalyi, PhD (pronounced me-high chick-sent-me-high) explains in his article <u>The Creative Personality: Ten paradoxical traits of the creative personality</u> (from his book Creativity: Flow and the Psychology of Discovery and Invention) that "Creative people tend to be smart yet naive at the same time."

He says that "a core of general intelligence is high among people who make important creative contributions," but according to the studies of Lewis Terman, "after a certain point IQ does not seem to be correlated with superior performance in real life" – including level of creative expression.

Csikszentmihalyi notes that Howard Gardner "remarked in his study of the major creative geniuses of this century, a certain immaturity, both emotional and mental, can go hand in hand with deepest insights."

Gardner's book is <u>Creating Minds: An Anatomy of Creativity as Seen Through the Lives of Freud, Einstein, Picasso, Stravinsky, Eliot, Graham, and Gandhi</u>.

High intelligence and ability can include high challenges.

One of the themes I have noticed in the research on talent and creativity is that having so-called advanced potential, or being multitalented, does not confer any guarantee of success on any level, or any kind of "automatic" fulfillment of those abilities.

For example, Sally M. Reis, PhD of The National Research Center on the Gifted and Talented, notes in an article of hers (Internal barriers, personal issues, and decisions faced by gifted and talented females) that high potential and multiple interests, multipotentiality, can benefit many women, but others "often cannot find their niche, make it on their own, or choose a vocational path."

That can apply to us men as well, of course.

Also see my article Is Intellect an Albatross? in which I explore the question of whether an exceptional mind has potential negative consequences, particularly for women.

In her Foreword to the book "Enjoying the Gift of Being Uncommon" by Willem Kuipers, Linda Silverman, PhD (Director of the Gifted Development Center) notes, "The vast majority of gifted adults are never identified. Even those who were tested as children and placed in gifted programs often believe that their giftedness disappeared by the time they reached adulthood.

"It does not seem to matter how much success a person achieves—hardly anyone is comfortable saying, 'I'm gifted.' That is why this book is such a major breakthrough."

She continues, "Willem Kuipers bypasses the problem by coining a much more palatable term: eXtra intelligent (Xi). And, if someone has a knee-jerk reaction to that idea, Xi can also stand for eXtra intense. More people are aware of and admit to their intensity than to their uncommon intelligence.

"Parents note the intensity of their young child before they realize that their child is developing at a faster rate. High intensity is a close cousin to high intelligence."

Read more quotes and info about the book in my High Ability site post The Gift of Being Uncommon.

It may be very helpful to look at your own ideas about intelligence and ability.

There is a lot of cultural influence about what constitutes ability and multiple talents - such as the endless media repetition of the "usual suspects" in the role model pantheon of exceptional achievers

So, if you aren't as adept or accomplished or well-known as Mozart,

Einstein or Georgia O'Keeffe, Bill Gates, Lady Gaga or Meryl Streep, you may tend to think you aren't "really" talented.

Being young and exceptional is often difficult.

A couple of teens writing in the book When Gifted Kids Don't Have All the Answers articulated some of this impact:
"Other kids made fun of us as nerds or called us stuck-up. It was not true, it was just that we weren't sure how to relate to some of our peers. We were informed that we were smarter by our teachers, but to a child, that is just plain 'different.' We needed help understanding ourselves." - Erin, 19
"Gifted kids tend to hide their intelligence, as well as their talents, for a very simple reason: Conformity." - Claudia, 16

We are infovores

Research shows we are infovores – that our brains crave new information. That is especially true for exceptional, multitalented people.
USC professor Irving Biederman investigates the neuroscience behind the infovore phenomenon, and has carried out

research showing that in "association areas" of the brain, where "sensory information triggers memory and taps into previous knowledge," there is a high density of opioid receptors, so we get pleasure when "a new piece of information tickles that part of your brain where you interpret the scene or conversation."

Continued in his article <u>The 411 to avoid boredom</u>.

Ø Ø Ø

OBSESSION - PERSEVERANCE

"Sometimes creativity is a compulsion, not an ambition."

- Actor Edward Norton (in Entertainment Weekly ew.com), about the documentary "The Devil and Daniel Johnston" (2006) – about a manic-depressive singer.

The language we use to ourselves and others about talents can have a big impact on our attitudes and motivation. For all too many years, I have been self-critical about focusing on creative interests instead of, for example, socializing.

But choices like that generally aren't simply right or wrong, though of course there are consequences.

Positive Obsessions fuel creative expression

Creativity coach Eric Maisel, PhD thinks obsession is a more or less necessary element of creative achievement - at least the healthy variety of obsession.

He says, "Negative obsessions are a true negative for everyone, but most creators — and all would-be creators — simply aren't obsessed enough. For an artist, the absence of positive obsessions leads to long periods of blockage, repetitive work that bores the artist himself, and existential ailments of all sorts."

From his article: In Praise of Positive Obsessions.

Perseverance and a rebellious spirit

A variation on obsession is "stubborness" or perseverance.

When she was a newly single mother and struggling to support her baby daughter in Edinburgh, J.K. Rowling chose to commit herself to her dream of becoming a novelist by writing "Harry Potter."

She admits feeling "very low" and having a need "to achieve something. Without the challenge, I would have gone stark raving mad."

[From article J.K. Rowling: A wizard of odds (Psychology Today).

See more comments by Rowling in my High Ability post: Celebrating our unique qualities.

Another Psychology Today article – Why Prodigies Fail – says that most childhood prodigies never fulfill their promise.

"Perseverance is a key part of it," says Robert Root-Bernstein of Michigan State University. "Many of them say that their expectations were warped by their early experiences."

The article notes, "When success comes too easily, prodigies are ill prepared for what happens when the adoration goes away, their competitors start to catch up and the going gets rough."

There can be a lesson here for any of us, not just prodigies.

(He is co-author with Michele Root-Bernstein of Sparks of Genius: The Thirteen Thinking Tools of the World's Most Creative People.

Indiana University psychologist Jonathan Plucker notes, "I don't see anyone teaching these kids about task commitment, about perseverance in the face of social pressures, about how to handle criticism.

"We say, 'Boy, you're really talented.' We don't say, 'Yeah, but you're still going to have to put in those 60-hour work weeks before you can make major contributions to your field.'"

(Jonathan A. Plucker is a co-author of Essentials of Creativity Assessment.)

Developing creativity with time, risk, love and hard work

Creative achievement - especially the sort that gets mentioned in books and the media - has often been considered something special, that only a "genius" can do. I have often felt held back in writing, such as this book, by self-limiting ideas related to how I identify myself and my writing talents.

Professor of psychology R. Keith Sawyer, among others, disputes that idea. He was asked, "What advice can you give us nongeniuses to help us be more creative?"

His answer: "Take risks, and expect to make lots of mistakes, because creativity is a numbers game. Work hard, and take frequent breaks, but stay with it over time. Do what you love, because creative breakthroughs take years of hard work. Develop a network of colleagues, and schedule time for freewheeling, unstructured discussions."

He added, "Most of all, forget those romantic myths that creativity is all about being artsy and gifted and not about hard work. They discourage us because we're waiting for that one full-blown moment of inspiration. And while we're waiting, we may never start working on what we might someday create."

From article The Hidden Secrets of the Creative Mind, Time mag. Jan. 8, 2006. Prof. Sawyer is author of Explaining Creativity: The Science of Human Innovation.

Mozart and so-called genius

In a New York Times op-ed, David Brooks pointed out that Mozart's early compositions "were nothing special. They were pastiches of other people's work."

He added, "Mozart was a good musician at an early age, but he would not stand out among today's top child-performers.

"What Mozart had, we now believe, was the same thing Tiger Woods had — the ability to focus for long periods of time and a father intent on improving his skills."

From his article Genius: The Modern View – which also includes a video about the book "<u>The Talent Code: Greatness Isn't Born. It's Grown. Here's How</u>" by Daniel Coyle.

Eminence and creative achievement

Previous research has confirmed that a high IQ in childhood is not a guarantee for eminence or creative productivity.

But in her article <u>Discovering the Gifted Ex-Child</u>, Stephanie S. Tolan notes that achievement - and giftedness itself - are open to different viewpoints.

She writes, "Not everyone perceives giftedness in the same way. Some see it as the achievement of something out of the ordinary, essentially external. Others see it as an internal set of out-of-the-ordinary mental processes that may or may not lead to achievement."

Grit and mastery and perseverance

Researchers within gifted education, and authors on adult talent assert that personality factors and motivation are the most important elements of creative achievement, and they distinguish creative producers from others.

In his article <u>The Winning Edge</u>, Peter Doskoch [Psychology Today] points out that with examples like Mozart, "We're primed to think that talent is the key to success. But what counts even more is a fusion of passion and perseverance. In a world of instant gratification, grit may yield the biggest payoff of all."

Malcolm Gladwell describes in his book Outliers: The Story of Success some of the personal and social aspects of how people become exceptional - "outliers" on the upper end of ability and achievement curves.

Based on multiple research studies, he declares that to master any skill requires about 10,000 concentrated hours of focus and persistence. "The Beatles were willing to play for eight hours straight, seven days a week," he notes as one example.

From my High Ability site post Outliers and developing exceptional abilities.

Ø Ø Ø

IDENTITY - EGO - SELF-ESTEEM - ECCENTRICITY

How do we effectively create out of our unique identity, without getting so attached to that identity we shut out new creative inspiration?

And can we gain fame for creative expression without becoming so ego-centered that we compromise the openness needed for creativity?

For most of my life I have struggled with unhealthy self-esteem and high self-criticism - but reading many books on giftedness and creativity, and interviews with talented and accomplished actors, directors, writers and other artists, I have come to realize that I am far from alone.

It seems to me these large topics of identity, ego etc. are interrelated.

Building identity without corroding our authenticity

Actor Catherine Keener, in an article about her movie "Capote," said she "understands how a perfectly nice person with a talent for acting, or directing, or music making builds a big career and in doing so loses much of who they were to begin with," as writer Mary McNamara put it [Los Angeles Times Dec 6, 2005].

"I see it happen with people I like," Keener says. "They feel manipulated, by the press, by the system, and they start to manipulate back. Like, 'OK, I'll do what you ask, but I want this and this and this.'"

But, she adds, "I want to shake them and say, 'What does it matter if you turn into someone you don't even like?' … It's so hard when that happens. When a friend crosses a line that maybe you didn't even know was there."

The "manipulating" behavior can be the kind of psychological coercion that Truman Capote employed when writing "In Cold Blood."

The movie, starring Philip Seymour Hoffman, was "about a man whose great achievement requires the surrender of his self-respect," as film critic Roger Ebert described it.

Playing the diva.

The comically exaggerated diva behavior of some movies or soap operas is one thing, but in real life it may be a form of self-destructive narcissism.

In a NY Times article [Acquired Situational Narcissism] Robert B. Millman, professor of psychiatry at Cornell Medical School, talks about the psychological dysfunction he identified.

He explains, "Psychoanalytic literature is filled with jargon about how narcissism happens really early, but I realized that given the right situation, it could happen much later.

"When a billionaire or a celebrity walks into a room, everyone looks at him. He's a prince. He has the power to change your life, and everyone is very conscious of that. So they're drawn to this person."

That might be just a description of leadership and charisma. The problem is when that attention changes the person.

What happens is that they get so used to everyone looking at them that they stop looking back at others, he says.

And, he adds, "They are different. They're not normal. And why would they feel normal when every person in the world who deals with them treats them as if they're not?"

Keeping narcissism in check

The late actor Heath Ledger recalled his mother seeing an early - and bad - acting performance of his, but not coddling him with false compliments about it: "No one else around you, except your mum, is going to tell you that you suck," he said.

He once said he thinks the problem with many actors in the industry is "We all just think we're brilliant, you know? And 98 per cent of us are crap. And we've got to realise that before we can improve." [London Observer, 02 April 2006]

But this isn't just about celebrity actors; narcissism is a complex psychological experience, and I'm only briefly mentioning it here.

Developing and using our creative talents can take many choices and compromises, but isn't losing touch with our authentic selves too big a price to pay for success?

Embracing our inner depths

The journey to our true identity and realizing our creative potential involves honestly looking at who and what we are on the inside, in our souls.

That can be uncomfortable, even painful for some people, but it is necessary for substantial personal growth and creative excellence.

It is a hero's journey and heroine's journey, not to be undertaken without courage. What lies within us can be chaotic and threatening, at least until we know ourselves enough to embrace who we really are.

Many people find ways to avoid looking into themselves deeply, or dealing with the discomforts of seeing. Maybe, in general, people who don't engage in that kind of inner awareness don't choose creative professions.

The fear of being authentic and unique

I have often admired prominent people in the arts who have unique, even flamboyant personalities and appearances, and seem, at least in public, to be courageously different. And one of my areas of self-limiting thinking is to say to myself something like, They must have had an upbringing or genes that lets them be so forthright and assertive.

But of course, as much as genes may play a role in personalty and anxiety, we are amazingly able to grow and change - if we are willing to face the fears in doing so.

In his book <u>The War of Art: Winning the Inner Creative Battle</u>, Steven Pressfield writes about our fear that we can transcend the mundane, to "become the person we sense in our hearts we truly are."

He thinks "This is the most terrifying prospect a human being can face," because it removes them (they imagine) from all the "tribal inclusions" their "psyche is wired for and has been for fifty million years."

And it is also about being exceptional. "We fear discovering that we are more than we think we are. More than our parents/children/ teachers think we are. We fear that we actually possess the talent that our still, small voice tells us. That we actually have the guts, the perseverance, the capacity."

What if you're superhuman?

One of the pleasures for me of the TV series "Heroes" was its depiction of, mostly, very real people with various superhuman, or meta-human, powers - and how they are facing themselves having such extraordinary abilities (stopping time; flying; foreseeing the future and more).

One of the heroes in the show, Hiro Nakamura (played by Masi Oka) says in one scene to his friend and fellow time-traveler Ando Masahashi (James Kyson Lee): "My only concern is should I hide my true identity? A costume maybe?"

To which Ando responds: "You start talking about capes and tights and I'm out of here."

It may be natural to be uncertain about our authentic inner selves, and want to shy away from it, or put on some kind of costume, physical or psychological.

According to various studies, that is a very real issue for gifted teens, who pretend they are not really as talented and capable as they, in fact are - so they can better fit in with their peers.

But, as personal development teacher Bob Proctor says in his article <u>Notes on The Secret DVD</u>, "You might not really believe in yourself, but if you keep studying, you are going to be absolutely amazed with yourself."

The fear of being worthy of our ideals but alone

In her stimulating newsletter [available by subscription at her site], Barbara Winter quotes from <u>The War of Art</u>: "We know that if we embrace our ideals, we must prove worthy of them. And that scares the hell out of us.

"What will become of us? We will lose our friends and family, who will no longer recognize us. We will wind up alone, in the cold void of starry space, with nothing and no one to hold on to."

She adds, "Of course this is exactly what happens. But here's the trick. We wind up in space, but not alone. Instead we are tapped into an unquenchable, undepletable, inexhaustible source of wisdom, consciousness, companionship."

She notes, "Yeah, we lose friends. But we find friends too, in places we never thought to look. And they're better friends, truer friends. And we're better and truer to them."

Barbara Winter affirms she has "been dazzled by the helpful, delightful, creative people that are in my life... If I ever doubted the Law of Attraction, I'd only have to scan my e-mailbox to see that I consistently attract people who are curious, adventurous and committed to making a difference."

In its superficial presentations, I think the so-called Law of Attraction is potentially misleading people into setting aside the needs to formulate and take action for your own growth and success.

But one of the most rewarding aspects of publishing my various sites and using Twitter and Facebook over the years, is just what she is talking about: I have connected with so many people who share interests in creative expression and personal development.

Exploring who we are through art

One way we have to understand ourselves more deeply is through literature, the arts and fantasy - not only consuming all those, but creating.

As Jungian writer Marie-Louise von Franz says in her book The Interpretation of Fairy Tales, "Fantasy is not just whimsical ego-nonsense but comes really from the depths; it constellates symbolic situations which give life a deeper meaning and a deeper realization."

Being eccentric and creative

"I hope I'm becoming more eccentric. More room in the brain."
Musician Tom Waits

I have enjoyed that quote for years. Being eccentric - choosing not to be more safely mundane - can help our creative thinking and courage.

As psychologist Robert Ornstein, PhD has noted, "If you spend too much time being like everybody else, you decrease your chances of coming up with something different." He is author of <u>The Psychology of Consciousness</u>.

Karl Lagerfeld, the prominent fashion designer, photographer and publisher, and artistic director of Chanel, has eclectic and unusual tastes in clothing - so I would consider him one example of an eccentric.

A profile article notes that in his home there is "a narrow room lined with shelves. On the top of a bureau were perhaps two hundred pairs of fingerless gloves, arranged in neat piles according to color (he explained that he chose the gray pair he's wearing because of the overcast sky).

"There are also dozens of pairs of jeans, and belts laid out by the hundred. Next door was a windowless room containing a dozen garment racks on wheels, each one stuffed with suits—perhaps five hundred in all—in black or gray hues."

Lagerfeld admits, "I have suits here I've never worn. To normal people it may look sick, huh?" He shrugged. "I don't know what 'normal' means, anyway."

[From In the Now - Where Karl Lagerfeld lives. By John Colapinto, New Yorker, March 19, 2007.]

Probably a number of people, including perhaps mental health professionals, would consider some of his behavior "sick" or neurotic. Some of what he said reminds me of the A&E TV program Hoarders, which "looks inside the lives whose inability to part with their belongings is so out of control that they are on the verge of a personal crisis."

Another example of an eccentric creative leader is mentioned by historian Daniel J. Boorstin, who says Beethoven's apartments numbered more than 60, as he kept moving on to a new one.

That item is from Boorstin's book Creators – a History of Heroes of the

Imagination – and quoted in my article Eccentricity and Creativity.

British neuropsychologist David Weeks studied and interviewed a wide range of such "daring and different" people for his book Eccentrics: A Study of Sanity and Strangeness, and concluded "One of the principal reasons eccentrics continually challenge the established order is because they want to experiment, to try out new ways of doing things."

And that may be one of the key benefits of being eccentric (which, of course, is often "in the eye of the beholder") - that it can open up your thinking to try out new and different approaches to creative challenges.

Tim Burton

His films are always satisfying and exciting to me on multiple levels. What are some of the aspects of Tim Burton's life and way of working that help him be so creative?

Costume designer Colleen Atwood also admires Burton as an artist, and explains: "He is able to open himself up to the world, through his own world, which is very unusual. His work has a very separate and personal voice and it comes from a very true place. At the same time it's incredibly entertaining."

Burton has commented on the importance of inner drive: "The tricky thing about being in the entertainment industry is that basically no matter how much money is involved, how good the life is, the thing that still compels you is that thing inside."

Read more quotes and see a video interview in my post Tim Burton on nurturing his unique creative vision.

Also see more quotes and books on the page Eccentricity.

Einstein and other non-conformists

In his Wired magazine article The World Needs More Rebels Like Einstein, Walter Isaacson notes that Einstein's concept that "time is relative depending on your state of motion" had been explored by other scientists, who "had come close to his insight, but they were too confined by the dogmas of the day. Einstein alone was impertinent enough to discard the notion of absolute time, one of the sacred tenets of classical physics since Newton."

Isaacson wrote the biography Einstein: His Life and Universe.

Albert Einstein expressed an insight on non-conforming when he said, "Few people are capable of expressing with equanimity opinions which differ from the prejudices of their social environment. Most people are even incapable of forming such opinions."

That quote affirms one of the main values of operating outside the norms which can restrict personal growth and creativity. Social environment is a pervasive influence on how we think and act. Even if you think you are past your high school worries about being accepted and "cool," there are pressures to stay on familiar and accepted paths.

The quote comes from the book by Neuropsychologist David Weeks I mentioned earlier: Eccentrics: A Study of Sanity and Strangeness, and Weeks lists many other people considered eccentrics, such as William Blake, Alexander Graham Bell, Emily Dickinson, Charlie Chaplin, Ludwig Wittgenstein, and Howard Hughes.

Hughes (portrayed so well by Leonardo DiCaprio in "The Aviator") was another "larger than life" personality who clearly had mental health issues, and yet made global impacts on the culture.

One of my points is that being "strange" or eccentric can be unhealthy, or can be more healthy than if we restrict ourselves to "normal" when we authentically have traits and abilities beyond the ordinary.

One of Einstein's characteristics, shared with many other eccentrics, was his "childlike propensity of the creative mind," Weeks writes.

Another example was artist William Blake, who was "often described by his contemporaries as being childlike."

Weeks notes that many computer experts or even hackers are eccentric: "Because of their innate ability to innovate and their penchant for the unorthodox, many young science jocks are are able to live a solitary, nocturnal life."

Some of those aspects help support being creative, but can also fuel the ethical distortions and costly destructiveness perpetrated by some criminal hackers.

The eccentric millionaire entrepreneur Dean Kamen

In her Scientific American magazine article The Unleashed Mind: Why Creative People Are Eccentric, creativity researcher Shelley Carson notes "People who are highly creative often have odd thoughts and behaviors—and vice versa. Both creativity and eccentricity may be the result of genetic variations that increase cognitive disinhibition —the brain's failure to filter out extraneous information."

"When unfiltered information reaches conscious awareness in the brains of people who are highly intelligent and can process this information without being overwhelmed, it may lead to exceptional insights and sensations."

She writes about "one of the world's best known and most successful entrepreneurs, with hundreds of patents to his name—including the Segway scooter. But you will never see Dean Kamen in a suit and tie: the eccentric inventor dresses almost exclusively in denim."

She also mentions other unusual behaviors: "He spent five years in college before dropping out, does not take vacations and has never married. Kamen presides (along with his Ministers of Ice Cream, Brunch and Nepotism) over the Connecticut island kingdom of North Dumpling, which has 'seceded' from the U.S. and dispenses its own currency in units of pi. Visitors are issued a visa form that includes spaces on which to note identifying marks on both their face and buttocks."

Sounds like a great work environment for eccentrics.

Carson has a number of perspectives on developing creative talents. Listen to my podcast interview with her: Shelley Carson on enhancing our creative brain, and see her book Your Creative Brain: Seven Steps to Maximize

So much social pressure to conform.

The book Gifted Grownups: the Mixed Blessings of Extraordinary Potential quotes researcher J.M.Tolliver, who has studied gifted and creative people, about the danger of not allowing non-conformity: "Of all the disservice we do our students, perhaps the most critical is demanding that they 'fit.' We are intolerant of deviant discretions, expelling those who do not learn their (conformity) lessons well… A cynicism develops concerning the generation of ideas."

Adults in authority are often "intolerant of deviant discretions" by students, such as expelling them for displaying 'inflammatory' t-shirts, or wearing head scarves, or showing up at school with an eyebrow trimmer because it could be a 'weapon.'

Being strange and eccentric can work for us as an artist

Actor Rex Lee plays agent assistant Lloyd on the HBO series "Entourage" – and says he has "always understood that I'm incredibly strange. And at some point in my life

I decided that I really liked myself the way I was.."

More on my <u>The Inner Actor</u> site.

Cecil Beaton [1904-80; fashion and portrait photographer, and stage and costume designer] encouraged actively being non-conforming: "Be daring, be different, be impractical; be anything that will assert integrity of purpose and imaginative vision against the play-it-safers, the creatures of the commonplace, the slaves of the ordinary."

Ego and eccentricity and creativity

Being uniquely yourself, even eccentric, can look to some people, at some times, like being egotistical or narcissistic - but I think those are not at all the same thing.

One sense of this word "ego" is a distorted self-regard, what psychologist Carl Jung referred to as "inflated consciousness... hypnotized by itself."

Responding to the question: "What kills creativity?", actress Gillian Anderson replied succinctly, "Ego."

Many people recognize the need to modulate this kind of ego in order to facilitate the creative process.

David Milch – creator, writer, and producer of the HBO series "Deadwood" among many other projects – commented in an interview about "trusting the process of the active imagination. It entails suppression of the Ego. I am able to develop exercises where I can suppress that quickly. I am able to get to the work faster every day."

He adds that he doesn't "linger a lot in self-delusory exercises in control – don't describe too much or even have to have an objective idea of what a scene is about. My only responsibility to an active imagination is to submit myself to a state of being where characters other than I move around and I try to serve that process."

He added, "I am content to work in uncertainty much more than I used to be – content to not know where I am going."

[From interview: David Milch's Active Imagination, by David Boles, Go Inside Magazine, May 17, 2002.]

Also see my related article on this topic: Ego and Creativity.

Ø Ø Ø

INTEGRITY

You can probably make notable creative achievements without much concern for integrity or being authentic, but many artists agree that respecting their personal values is a strong element in being successful and fulfilled as a creator.

Looking back on parts of my own life, I realize that not respecting my authentic values (and emotional needs), just to make money - as necessary as that is, of course - was often a strong element in my depression, anxiety and general disconnection with my personal power and joy, and ability to be creative.

Julie Delpy on filmmaking with integrity

Perhaps most well-known as an actor, Julie Delpy is also a writer, composer and director - and an example of an artist who values authenticity.

She says, "I am obsessed with integrity. Integrity, for me, comes before everything. And let me tell you, Hollywood is an industry where integrity is really a challenge. People underestimate the word 'prostitution.' Prostitution isn't reserved for people who walk the streets at night. In Hollywood, people of all ages and creeds succeed through prostitution. They succeed by selling out."

She continues, "My point isn't to be negative, but to be realistic about what the challenges are... Hollywood movies set the tone for our culture—and it's so important to create films where men and women are represented as full people, not objects or caricatures."

From Delpy's blog post <u>Succeed by Selling Out? I think not</u> on the site of Imagining Ourselves, an exhibition of the International Museum of Women.

That idea of "selling out" of course applies to other creative arenas like book publishing: Are you compromising your integrity to go along with a publisher who 'suggests' you include a character or element that you don't agree with, or feel uncomfortable about?

Or what about changing the dominant color of your artwork, such as a painting, to better match the interior decor of a customer's home or office?

The point is not that all outside 'suggestions' are wrong for a creative project, only that they should be considered in light of your values as a creator.

Ø Ø Ø

AUTONOMY

As creative, uncommon people we may usually have a need for independence and control over our lives. Being self-directed and self-defined are common traits of creatively talented and exceptional people, but there may often be internal and external influences that compromise that autonomy.

Mary-Elaine Jacobsen [author of The Gifted Adult] notes in her article Giftedness in the Workplace that gifted adults "may fail to respect their own need for solitude, reflection, and time to daydream or play with concepts and ideas. They may shame themselves when their strong bids for autonomy result in a pattern of butting heads with authority figures."

A need for solitude is also a component of the personality trait of high sensitivity - see more on the trait in the chapter on the topic.

"The successful person seeks autonomy."

Earl Nightingale [founder of personal development company Nightingale-Conant] says in his article Life of the Unsuccessful, "More than any other factor, perhaps, the unsuccessful person can usually be identified with a group that is at the mercy of events. The successful person seeks autonomy and makes his or her own plans and has the self-esteem and inner excitement and knowledge to know that those plans can be followed."

Feeling in control

In his article "Hey, grads: Have you figured out the rest of your life yet?" [usatoday.com 6/11/2006], Chris Ballard notes that people want to feel in control, and notes, "While researching a book about people who are very good at unusual jobs , I found something grads would be wise to consider: the perception of autonomy is often more powerful than actual autonomy. The people I spent time with — characters that included a 'lumberjill' and a wall-walking repairman — were often fine with their long hours and the way their professions at times consumed their lives. The reason: They felt they were doing the work of their own free will."

Ballard's book is The Butterfly Hunter : Adventures of People Who Found Their True Calling Way Off the Beaten Path.

The site Changing Course by Dr. Valerie Young has a variety of programs, books, and workshops for "off the beaten path" jobs and careers. Titles include: Making Dreams Happen; Finding Your True Calling; Creative Alternatives to Having a J-o-b. Also see my Inner Entrepreneur site post Valerie Young on turning your interests into income.

Ø Ø Ø

HIGH SENSITIVITY

Are creative people unusually sensitive? A variety of both clinical experience and research reports confirm that is often true. And many creative people report examples from their own experience that indicate they have this personality trait - more technically called sensory processing sensitivity.

It is only in the past few years that I have 'discovered' this trait, and realized how much it applies to me and helps explain a number of reactions I have had to people and the world in general - reactions that for a long time I considered 'weird' and perhaps more symptoms of mental health imbalance.

Psychotherapist Lisa A. Riley, LMFT comments: "Throughout my practice, I have encountered a connection between highly sensitive people and their own creative impulses. This characteristic does not discriminate between painter, actor, or musician—they all appear to have one thing in common: they experience the world differently than the average individual."

She adds, "Creatives often feel and perceive more intensely, dramatically, and with a wildly vivid color palate to draw from, which can only be described as looking at the world through a much larger lens."

From her article: <u>Highly Sensitive Personality and Creativity</u>.

One of the leading authors and researchers on high sensitivity is Elaine Aron, PhD, who has detailed the trait in a number of books including <u>The Highly Sensitive Person.</u>

Giftedness and sensitivity

In one of her newsletter articles, Dr. Aron talks about the differences between giftedness and sensitivity, in both children and adults.

She wrote, "Aside from the considerable problem of just defining giftedness or even intelligence (for example, is it global or is any talent a gift or form of intelligence?), I have resisted viewing sensitivity in these highly positive ways for three reasons. First, in my experience, not all gifted people are highly sensitive. I know too many non-HSPs (highly sensitive persons) who are highly gifted. In fact, I wonder whether each temperament trait, at its extreme, might yield a type of gift.

"For example, my brilliant non-HSP husband is extremely persistent. He works on a problem until he solves it. Period. Surely that is a gift of a different type, but what a 'rage to master.' Or how about those non-HSP high sensation seekers? They explore endlessly and seek novelty and novel solutions—surely that makes them or some of them creative, or appear to be."

She continues that in her experience, not all highly sensitive people are gifted as adults, since many HSPs "are not expressing some talent in a way that others would recognize as outstanding.

"Further, most people like to think of giftedness as special and rare, saying it only occurs or should be said to occur in 1, 3, or 5% of the population. If one accepted that definition, all HSPs definitely could not be gifted. High sensitivity occurs in 15 to 20%. Finally, third, I think I did not even consider equating it with giftedness, intelligence, reflectiveness, awareness, or other positive spins because I wanted a neutral name for the trait. I also wanted it to apply to all levels of the body, from skin and immune system to neocortex, and to all species, from fruit fly to human."

But, she admits, "Of course 'sensitive' is not a neutral term either. Indeed, I wonder if there are any terms that are truly neutral to everyone. But at least its positive and negative connotations seem to be balanced!"

Continued in her article The Highly Sensitive Child (and Adults, Too): Is Sensitivity the Same as Being Gifted?

Sensitivity and creativity

In another comment, Dr. Aron said she knows "ALL HSPs are creative, by definition. "Many have squashed their creativity because of their low self-esteem; many more had it squashed for them, before they could ever know about. But we [HSPs] all have it." She adds, "One of the best ways to make life meaningful for an HSP is to use that creativity."

Meaning is another central topic related to creativity and multiple talents - see the chapter in this book.

The value of emotional sensitivity

If you are highly sensitive, you tend to notice more of your outer and inner environments, and process more sensory information. All of which can help make us more creative. Some areas of creative expression are especially appropriate and supportive for emotional sensitivity, an aspect of the trait for many people.

One area is acting. Nicole Kidman, for example, has noted she was a highly sensitive child, "and the last thing my parents wanted was for their child to go in and get hurt...Most actors are highly sensitive people, but you have this incredible scrutiny. You have to develop a thick skin, but you can't have a thick skin in your work."

[From my Inner Actor post Nicole Kidman on fame, and actors as highly sensitive people.]

In one of my videos, I include quotes by and about Winona Ryder, Heath Ledger, Amy Brenneman, Scarlett Johansson, Anne Hathaway, and Ellen DeGeneres about their experience of sensitivity. See the post: Video: On Being Sensitive.

Also see other posts on my Highly Sensitive site, and links to multiple articles and to sites of coaches who help highly sensitive people flourish and become more self-realized and creative.

Ø Ø Ø

INTENSITY

A related aspect - that may often accompany sensitivity - is high intensity. This is another trait that earlier in my life led me to think I was "crazy" - partly because it was an inner experience I had not read about or heard others talk about, and it is in many ways private. You can see some forms of expression of intensity in many actors and musicians - but, I suppose, I tended to think of it as being passionate or energetic.

As mentioned in the chapter on Intelligence, the book "Enjoying the Gift of Being Uncommon" by Willem Kuipers uses the term Xi for uncommon people, which can stand for eXtra intelligent, or eXtra intense. High ability people often, even typically, have personality characteristics that include high intensity or excitability.

Polish psychiatrist and psychologist Kazimierz Dabrowski developed a theory of personality and emotional development that is often applied toward understanding the psychology of extra intelligent and intense, gifted and talented individuals. One aspect of his Theory of Positive Disintegration is the concept of unusual intensity and reactivity, which he called overexcitability.

In their book <u>Living With Intensity: Understanding the Sensitivity, Excitability, and the Emotional Development of Gifted Children, Adolescents, and Adults</u>, Susan Daniels and Michael M. Piechowski explain, "Overexcitability is a translation of the Polish word which means 'superstimulatability.' (It should have been called superexcitability.) … Another way of looking at is of being spirited – 'more intense, sensitive, perceptive, persistent, energetic'…It would be hard to find a person of talent who shows little evidence of any of the five overexcitabilities."

But they also note that many people may not welcome such traits: "Unfortunately, the stronger these overexcitabilities are, the less peers and teachers welcome them."

From my post <u>The psychology of creativity: performers and excitabilities</u>.

For more about those qualities, see the posts:

<u>Excitabilities and Gifted People – an intro by Susan Daniels</u>

<u>Dabrowski Excitabilities – Michael Jackson</u>

and my site: <u>Highly Sensitive</u>.

Don't tone it down

In her article (on my site) <u>Creative People Shouldn't 'Tone It Down'</u>, writer, writing coach, teacher, and speaker Cynthia Morris notes, "I've been accused of being 'too much' all my life. Too loud, too fast, too smart, too multi-talented, too audacious. I've never been able to live according to that external standard of 'just right'. Artists are often 'too much'. It's the job of the artist and writer to reflect what they see and feel. This expression of their art and talents must be larger than life. The trouble is, our expression doesn't always jibe with what's going on in the 'normal' world."

Do you ever "stifle yourself" to more easily get along with that 'normal' world? I certainly do - but it can be an emotionally costly choice, and one that inhibits creative energy and expression.

Using intensity and pain

Cheryl Arutt, Psy.D., a licensed clinical psychologist specializing in creative artist issues among topics, notes that "Creating art has always been a way to channel emotional intensity."

She points out we live in a world "where destructive acting out is all too frequent (and meticulously documented and sensationalized on the news and TMZ), sublimating painful feelings by expressing them in the form of artistic expression allows the artist to choose to 'act out' in a way that is constructive."

She adds, "Many creative people carry the belief that their pain is the locus of their creativity, and worry that they will lose their creativity if they work through their inner conflicts or let go of suffering. These artists hold onto their pain as if it were a lifeline, even finding ways to enhance it, leading to some patterns of behavior that won't 'turn off' even when they want them to."

The challenge for creative and intense people, she explains, is "Finding ways to maintain that optimal zone where we are neither under- or over-stimulated" which "allows us to use our minds to respond rather than to react. If you are an artist, you are your instrument. The greater access you maintain to yourself, the richer and broader your array of creative tools."

Musician Sting commented in the documentary All We Are Saying: "Do I have to be in pain to write? I thought so, as most of my contemporaries did; you had to be the struggling artist, the tortured, painful, poetic wreck. I tried that for a while, and to a certain extent that was successful. I was 'The King of Pain' after all. I only know that people who are getting into this archetype of the tortured poet end up really torturing themselves to death."

That is a quote I added to one of Dr. Arutt's guest articles on my site: <u>Affect Regulation and the Creative Artist</u>. Also see another article of hers: <u>The Artist's Unconscious</u>.

Ø Ø Ø

SEXUALITY

"Creativity is ultimately sexual."

In her article <u>Creative Juice - A Dozen Key Lessons for Creative Dreamers</u>, Suzanne Falter-Barns quotes Deepak Chopra: "Creativity is ultimately sexual – I'm sorry – but it is!"

Falter-Barns adds, "I couldn't agree more. I'd always had this sense that self-expression, passion and the stirrings of your soul were intertwined."

Do you agree? I think many of us would.

Writer Eve Ensler has commented that she believes "sexuality is the greatest gift we've been given. Its energy is the basis of creativity, love, ambition, desire, life. Sexuality has gotten all these bad raps because it's so powerful." [Quote from the book: Positive Energy by Judith Orloff, MD.]

Garry Trudeau, the creator of "Doonesbury," recalls an incident from his teens that illustrates that power: "As I was walking out the building one day on my lunch break, two-thirds of a block away this spectacularly beautiful young woman in a very short miniskirt was walking toward me. She was in her early twenties. I was 16 and looked all of 12. You could feel it in the air, her coming at you. Her presence was destabilizing the street for a one-block radius. Guys were gawking, cars were slowing. This woman was a menace."

He continues, "She was walking in a confident way, with a swing to her hips. I was geeky and shy, too shy to make eye contact. I wouldn't even have known what to DO with eye contact. My discomfort must have been obvious because, as she passes me, she leans over, her breath is warm, and she softly… growls in my ear. I thought to myself: I've just been handed the most extraordinary gift. She showed such wisdom, with such a generous use of power. She just changed the life of a young boy. I thought, Anything is possible." [Washington Post Magazine, Oct 22 2006]

Even a brief overview of the history of art shows how much romantic passion, sexuality, or appreciation of the 'opposite sex' in various ways has inspired artists, both male and female.

Painter Cecily Brown has been very articulate about sexuality in her work, and has commented, "I'm reluctant to say I want to capture the sensation of sex, but in a way, I want to transcribe the feeling of heat inside your body, inside your mouth, the feeling of skin on skin, and flesh and graspings. The subject is perfect for painting; painting is a metaphor for sex. So I want it caressing; I want it brutal and tender and everything at once." [From a contemporaryfinearts.de profile]

Ø Ø Ø

AWARENESS - INTUITION

"I feel there are two people inside me - me and my intuition. If I go against her, she'll screw me every time, and if I follow her, we get along quite nicely."

–Kim Basinger [imdb.com]

Making use of our talents and creative abilities depends on being relatively unhampered by constricting or distorting emotions and thinking - and having a more fluid and open awareness.

At periods of my life, for example, when I was really depressed or anxious, I was definitely not able to be particularly creative, or even think clearly about creative ideas.

Being creative isn't a matter of stopping our intellect, as writer Susan K. Perry, PhD notes, "I don't believe that when you get into a creative place, you're giving up thinking. You're super-thinking — better and with more parts of your mind than you do normally." [From my article Creativity and Flow Psychology.]

Dr. Perry is author of the book Writing In Flow, and you can hear my podcast interview with her at: Susan K. Perry, Ph.D. on writing.

Awareness, Neuroplasticity and Buddhist Psychology

Buddhism or Buddhist psychology promises learning and strategies to realize a kind of super-thinking and life balance.

Writer Charles Johnson once said that if it were not for the Buddhadharma (teachings),

"I'm convinced that, as a black American and an artist, I would not have been able to successfully negotiate my last half century of life in this country. Or at least not with a high level of creative productivity." [From his book Turning the Wheel : Essays on Buddhism and Writing]

The Dalai Lama, along with a number of Buddhist monks and leading neuroscientists, gather yearly at a conference about discoveries in the field of neuroplasticity: the study of how the human brain can change itself.

In her book Train Your Mind, Change Your Brain: How a New Science Reveals Our Extraordinary Potential to Transform Ourselves, Sharon Begley writes about this dynamic interaction of seemingly different areas of knowledge: "Buddhism has taught for twenty-five hundred years that the mind is an independent force that can be harnessed by will and attention to bring about physical change."

She quotes Francisca Cho: "The discovery that thinking something produces effects just as doing something does is a fascinating consonance with Buddhism, which challenges the traditional belief in an external, objective reality. Instead, it teaches that our reality is created by our own projections; it is thinking that creates the external world beyond us. The neuroscience findings harmonize with this Buddhist teaching."

Begley adds, "Indeed, Buddhism believes that the mind has a formidable power of self-transformation. When thoughts come to the untrained mind, they can run wild, triggering destructive emotions such as craving and hatred. But mental training, a core of Buddhist practice, allows us 'to identify and to control emotions and mental events as they arise,' says Matthieu Ricard."

French-born Buddhist monk Ricard further says that "If we place all our hopes and fears in the outside world, we have quite a challenge, because our control of the outside world is weak, temporary, and even illusory. It is more within the scope of our faculties to change the way we translate the outside world into inner experience. We have a great deal of freedom in how we transform that experience, and that is the basis for mental training and transformation… Buddhism defines a person as a constantly changing dynamic stream."

I really like that concept: a "dynamic stream" - it relates to other perspectives in this book about creative talent not being some kind of 'gift' from the outside, but an expression of our complex, always changing beings.

Some related books:

The Biology Of Belief by Bruce H. Lipton, PhD

"Don't believe everything you hear – even in your own mind." Daniel G. Amen, MD – author of Change Your Brain, Change Your Life – quoted in the book The Success Principles – by Jack Canfield

Changing our awareness

One form of changing our consciousness or emotions is using drugs. Alcohol and pot work. I've used both, earlier in my life. But as a means to enhance creativity, drugs and other substances are pretty limited and so potentially self-destructive. See more in the chapter on addiction.

But there are other approaches to changing consciousness.

Can hypnosis enhance creativity?

In his article Writers Thrive On Anxiety, hypno-psychotherapist Dr. Bryan Knight declares that hypnosis can help writers in a number of ways – helpful for other artists as well as writers, of course: "First, in lowering anxiety, second, in dealing with our own negative self-talk, third, in providing motivation to stop procrastinating, fourth, in building self-confidence (hypnotherapy is excellent in that regard), fifth, in releasing the creative power of the subconscious."

He quotes Ralph Keyes, author of The Courage to Write: "Many authors enter a trance-like state as they write. Distractions disappear. Anxiety is put on hold. After what seem like minutes, writers glance at the clock and see they've been working for hours. Writers often end a working session unable to recall a word they've written."

In his article Creative self hypnosis, painter Robert Genn talks about using techniques from experiments with students at the Architectural Foundation in London, England, including "trance-inducing music."

In another article Hypnosis Can Spawn Unlimited Creativity, Clinical Hypnotherapist Steve G. Jones explains that hypnosis "works to relax an individual to the point that ideas and images can be suggested and put to use.. to think in more creative terms. This works because the signals and messages that spark creative thinking are already within the person. It is just a matter of relaxing the mind to the point that they are unleashed." He offers a number of MP3 programs such as Unlimited Creativity Self Hypnosis.

There are many other producers and authors in the field of hypnotherapy, such as acclaimed psychologist Milton H. Erickson. One of his books is <u>Experiencing Hypnosis: Therapeutic Approaches to Altered States</u>.

My experience with hypnotherapy is limited to just a few sessions, but I found it to be relaxing, anxiety-reducing and a way to enhance mental focus. Using guided meditation or visualization may be considered related approaches. I regularly use a short (10 minute) free sample <u>Alpha Break audio download</u> guided meditation and relaxation program from Effective Learning Systems. Also, I use the Holosync CD for deep relaxation and meditation - for more about it see my Personal Growth Information site page <u>Centerpointe Research Institute mental fitness technology</u>.

Psychotherapist Sarah Chana Radcliffe has used Holosync audio CDs for years to benefit herself and her clients, and says, "I make it as a suggestion to clients who are experiencing stress, who are very anxious, or just need a fresh reworking of the brain." [From my post <u>Psychotherapist Sarah Chana Radcliffe on technologies for growth</u>.]

Also see a list of <u>Meditation and mindfulness articles</u> for enhancing creativity, emotional health and achievement.

Eric Maisel on creative mindfulness

Creativity coach and therapist Eric Maisel notes the word mindfulness stands for "the nonjudgmental observation and acknowledgment of our thoughts. We notice the thought – for example, 'I am running from my writing' – and acknowledge that we had the thought. The thought comes, we notice it, and it goes."

So, how is that relevant or useful for creative work? In my experience, one of the ways I have limited my creative expression is through identifying too much with my rational thought, and elevating it as the primary "authority" in making choices. As opposed to intuition, for example.

Maisel explains, "The central goal of ordinary mindfulness is to let such thoughts come and go without experiencing pain, without holding onto them, and without turning them into monsters that eat us alive."

But the goal of creative mindfulness, he says, is "not only the nonjudgmental observation of your thoughts but complete right thinking that leads to authenticity, creativity, and mental health. The high ideal of creative mindfulness is to master ordinary mindfulness, in the sense in which Jon Kabat-Zinn, Thich Nhat Hanh, and others have described it, and to employ that mastery in the service of deep thought, rich action, and wide-awake living."

Maisel enumerates six strategies of creative mindfulness, including:

"Fearlessly observe your thoughts. All of your excuses, all the ways you unhinge yourself, all of your dodges, all of your secret complaints and sources of pain, are right there in the thoughts you are thinking. Awaken to the knowledge of your own thoughts.

"Free your neurons, empty your mind, and ready yourself for creating. Ordinary mindfulness is the observation of thought. Creative mindfulness requires that you vanish, your mind hushed, so that your creative thoughts can appear. Open to an ever-deepening silence that is pregnant with your coming creative work."

From article: Mindfulness, by Eric Maisel, PhD.

Schizotypy

As tormenting and devastating as it is, schizophrenia may also include qualities of thinking that enhance creativity – qualities we may all experience, even if we aren't psychotic.

In his post Schizotypy, Flow, and the Artist's Experience, Scott Barry Kaufman, Ph.D. notes that schizotypy, a milder version of schizophrenia, "consists of a constellation of personality traits that are evident in some degree in everyone. Research confirms a link between schizotypy and creative achievement."

From my post Creative Thinking and Schizophrenia.

Eckhart Tolle on the creative potential of 'not knowing'

Author and spiritual teacher Eckhart Tolle also writes about mindful awareness, and suggests becoming at ease with the state of "not knowing." He says, "This takes you beyond mind because the mind is always trying to conclude and interpret. It is afraid of not knowing. So, when you can be at ease with not knowing, you have already gone beyond the mind. A deeper knowing that is non-conceptual then arises out of that state. Artistic creation, sports, dance, teaching, counseling — mastery in any field of endeavor implies that the thinking mind is either no longer involved at all or at least is taking second place."

From his article: Don't Take Your Thoughts Too Seriously.

Can trusting our intuition enhance creativity?

"You have to become very still and listen while your inner voice -- the very essence of you -- tells you who you are. You'll know you've found it when every cell in your body practically vibrates; when you're filled up by what you're doing instead of being drained by it."
– Oprah Winfrey [Intuition Newsletter, Aug 2004, by Lynn Robinson.]

Many writers extol the virtues of intuition for developing creative talents as well as making life decisions.

A research study by University College London indicates you are more likely to perform well on a symbol discrimination task if "you do not think too hard and instead trust your instincts," according to their press release article, Trusting your instincts leads you to the right answer.

Dr Li Zhaoping, of the UCL Department of Psychology, said: "If our higher-level and lower-level cognitive processes are leading us to the same conclusions, there is no issue. Often though, our instincts and higher-level functions are in conflict and in this case our instincts are often silenced by our reasoning conscious mind. Participants would have improved their performance if they had been able to switch off their higher-level cognition by, for example, acting quickly."

Another perspective is provided by Malcolm Gladwell, author of the book <u>Blink: The Power of Thinking Without Thinking</u> – he says what we refer to as intuition may be a matter of "rapid cognition" and thinks intuition strikes him "as a concept we use to describe emotional reactions, gut feelings — thoughts and impressions that don't seem entirely rational."

But, he adds, "I think that what goes on in that first two seconds is perfectly rational. It's thinking — its just thinking that moves a little faster and operates a little more mysteriously than the kind of deliberate, conscious decision-making that we usually associate with 'thinking.' What is going on in inside our heads when we engage in rapid cognition?"

In his book, he also points out failures of rapid cognition, describing cases where this sort of snap judgment thinking has resulted in significant, costly even deadly errors. Gladwell asserts that the process of rapid cognition is unconscious, so it may be affected by potentially distorting material such as prejudices and emotional wounds.

In his review of the book "Malcolmn Gladwell's Blink: Your First Impression Is Usually Correct in Complex Situations," technical writer Tom Johnson describes how he uses intuition or rapid cognition. "When I write a new post, essay, blurb, or other text, I usually have an immediate gut feeling as to whether it's good or bad. Sure I could tear apart my judgment by analyzing all the elements: Does it have a thought-provoking idea, evidence for the assertion, transitions between paragraphs, coherence? But really this careful analysis is only an attempt to understand or justify the initial instinct."

He also mentions how he responded to and judged others' writing: "When I was a composition teacher, I immediately knew, after reading a student essay, whether it was good or bad. It only took about one or two paragraphs to make this judgment. Of course in my end comment, I had to justify my judgment, writing comments related to qualities I mentioned above. But I never proceeded through a list of characteristics to measure an essay before arriving at a conclusion of its worth."

This is something I have noticed in evaluating my own writing as well - sometimes it just immediately "feels right" so I try to keep my critical mind at bay so it won't try to find something wrong with it.

Dismissive of intuition

It can be a challenge for people who are predominantly intellectual to acknowledge and make use of intuition.

Linda Kreger Silverman, PhD (Director of the Gifted Development Center) notes, "Individuals with higher intelligence are likely to be well educated. Higher education indoctrinates students to think logically and skeptically and to dismiss intuitive information. Scientific evidence and logical argument are considered legitimate, whereas intuitive knowing and higher wisdom are relegated to the realm of superstition."

She continues, "It is difficult for highly educated, gifted adults to trust their intuitive insights, to discuss them openly and to write about them for fear of losing credibility within the scientific community. Gifted people have often felt that they needed to align themselves professionally with either science or intuition."

But using our intuition isn't simply a matter of always trusting it, and assuming it must be valid.

In his article Intuition or Intellect, David G. Myers notes, "My geographical intuition tells me that Reno is east of Los Angeles and that Rome is south of New York. But I am wrong." He quotes Nobel Prize-winning physicist Richard Feynman: "The first principle is that you must not fool yourself — and you are the easiest person to fool."

From my High Ability site post <u>Gifted adults: Wrestling with our intuition</u>.

Still, many writers and personal development coaches say that respecting our gut feelings and intuitive thinking can help access creativity and lead us toward more fulfillment of our talents.

Is being a cynic reasonable, or self-defeating?

"It's hard to argue against cynics – they always sound smarter than optimists because they have so much evidence on their side."
Columnist Molly Ivins (1944-2007).

That is a quote from a Psychology Today article: <u>A Field Guide to the Cynic</u>, By Elizabeth Svoboda. She quotes from Rick Bayan's site <u>The Cynic's Sanctuary</u>: "The world belongs to people with IQs of 120. Anything much greater or less amounts to a liability." The site identifies itself as a home for "disgruntled idealists, subversive wits, professional misfits, skeptical jesters, curmudgeons, and misanthropes."

An aside here: Do you identify yourself with any of those labels?

How does our self-concept relate to our attitudes about other people, about the challenges we may have in expressing our talents, or the possibilities for doing meaningful work?

Svoboda notes that "when he was a newly minted history graduate, Bayan was convinced his knowledge of ancient wars and English monarchs would lead to a creative, lucrative job. Bayan's first dead-end gigs, editing obscure trade publications like Rubber Age and Container News, were enough to start the pessimistic wheels turning in his brain. He became moody and depressed, apt to deliver angry retorts to anyone who got in his way… his disillusionment, depression, and hostility (along with defensive pessimism) all form the constellation of traits that make up the cynic."

Are disillusionment & loss of creative potential linked?

Svoboda says University of California-Irvine personality researcher Salvatore Maddi contends that many cynics are like Bayan, and aren't so much born as made. "According to Maddi," she writes, "the first seeds of cynicism are often planted when people put in effort to achieve a goal like snagging a promotion at work or raising a self-sufficient child—and then see their high hopes dashed."

Svoboda adds that a hallmark of the cynical personality, or response, is the sense that nothing one does in life really matters.

This sort of helplessness is a feature of depression, too.

Clinical psychologist Michael Yapko says, "While cynical people are at no greater risk for depression, those who ruminate on their pessimistic thoughts are."

That has certainly been true for me: in my years of experiencing depression and dysthymia, rumination has often "kept it going" when thinking about other aspects of my life more might have lightened my moods.

Cynics can count some noteworthy examples, such as Friedrich Nietzsche, Dorothy Parker, and Oscar Wilde.

Svoboda's article also quotes Philip Mirvis, a cynicism researcher at Boston College, who says cynics' caustic, detached outlook on life, also known as defensive pessimism, helps "protect them from what they imagine to be the slings and arrows of hustlers and higher-ups."

Maybe a less than glowingly optimistic attitude can help buffer us against the various forms of rejection that creative expression so often entails.

For one of many articles related to attitude, see A Recipe for Authentic Living: Making Meaning, by Eric Maisel, PhD.

Ø Ø Ø

MATURITY

One of my self-limiting attitudes in the past was along the lines of "I'm getting too old to pursue x" - whether 'x' was acting, taking up a musical instrument again, writing magazine articles, developing websites or a number of endeavors. After dabbling in acting as an extra on a few movies, I decided that wasn't where my creative interests were. But age is not really an issue for most endeavors.

There are certainly forms of creative expression that depend on physical agility and training which can be developed more easily and successfully at younger ages, but there is no particular age limit when you can't pursue most creative interests.

"Nobody wants to leave the party."

In addition to many other projects, Candice Bergen at age 60 was a dynamic part of the ensemble of actors on the TV series "Boston Legal" and once commented, "A decade ago, I figured making it to 85 would be great. A vital 85. Then I thought, screw that. I'm going to live to 90. A vital 90… No, it still sucks. Living to 85's not okay; living to 90's not okay. Nobody wants to leave the party."

She also commented in a 2005 AARP mag. article, "People sometimes get crazier as they get older. I can just be weird whenever I want, and there's the freedom of not caring what people think."

Getting 'crazier' can be part of being more creative. Bergen was probably referring to being more eccentric - see the chapter on "Identity - Ego - Self Esteem - Eccentricity." But even more 'crazy' mentality may help enhance creativity, such as Schizotypy - see the chapter "Awareness - Thinking - Intuition."

But back to maturity. Architect Oscar Niemeyer received the highest honor in his field, the Pritzker Prize, months after his 80th birthday, and at age 97 was developing one of his most ambitious projects, a mile-long seafront esplanade of buildings and open space in Brazil.

Stan Lee is a writer, editor, actor, producer, publisher, television personality, and the former president and chairman of Marvel Comics - and still going strong at age 89. His Stan Lee Foundation was founded to focus on literacy, education and the arts.

Samuel Ullman (1840-1924) wrote his poetic essay "Youth" in his seventies: "Youth is not a time of life – it is a state of mind. It is not a matter of red cheeks, red lips and supple knees. It is a temper of the will; a quality of the imagination; a vigor of the emotions; it is a freshness of the deep springs of life. Youth means a temperamental predominance of courage over timidity, of the appetite for adventure over a life of ease. This often exists in someone of fifty, more than in a boy or girl of twenty. Nobody grows old by merely living a number of years; people grow old by deserting their ideals."

[Slightly paraphrased, from Alabama Moments site.]

But maintaining our vigor and vitality to be able to stay vital and creating into later life is not automatic. There is a great deal of very promising anti-aging research that is encouraging. One area is supplements: I have been using a variety of them for years, and notice benefits (such as almost no colds, and more stable moods than I had earlier in my life). I have listed a number of products on the Supplements page on my site.

Surviving maturity – and creatively thriving

Aging can bring a needed evaluation of our inner and outer lives, and perhaps some breaking down of barriers to our creative potential.

Playwright Edward Albee achieved early career success ("The Zoo Story," "Who's Afraid of Virginia Woolf?,") that was followed by several decades of "thorny obscurity and neglect," but a triumphant return to achievement in his mid-70s with his Tony-winning play "The Goat, or Who Is Sylvia?", according to a 2003 SF Chronicle article listing other enduring creators: Survival as art: 20 who defied the odds to follow their muse.

Jane Fonda at 73 is active in many entertainment and social activism projects. On the Joy Behar TV show she talked about living dynamically into maturity, and advised: "Understand what you're supposed to do with your life." Fonda (referring to Suzanne Braun Levine's idea of the "fertile void") says, "You're going through a real crisis, but it's also very fertile…you're very, very vulnerable. But if you can come through that to the other side, it can be the most wonderful part of life."

Her audiobook: Prime Time.

A rough passage

Sara Davidson, author of LEAP! What Will We do with the Rest of our Lives?, wrote in her Huffington Post entry The Narrows about what can be a "rough passage to the next part of life. In the Narrows, you feel you're being stripped of your identity and your worth. I sank into the narrows in my fifties."

She explains, "After 24 years of writing for TV, I couldn't get hired anymore, my partner left abruptly, and my kids went off to college. I spent two years thrashing, trying to get back what I'd lost, before I surrendered to the reality that my former life was finished and I couldn't know what the hell was ahead."

But, she notes, "There's a new life stage–after 50 and before 80–and we're the ones whose mission it will be to figure out what to do with it."

One of the people she interviewed for her book was political activist Tom Hayden (born in 1939). She notes on her site www.saradavidson.com that "After 18 years in the California legislature, he lost a municipal election to a man half his age, suffered heart failure and had a quintuple bypass, followed by depression. Now he's forging a new role, teaching and inspiring young people to work in politics."

She goes on to quote Hayden: "We can be freer now than we've been since we were 20. We may have 30 more years to give the system hell!"

A profile of him on his site tomhayden.com says he "writes for The Nation and organizes, travels and speaks constantly against the current wars as founder and Director of the Peace and Justice Resource Center" and "is still a leading voice for ending the wars in Afghanistan, Iraq, and Pakistan, for erasing sweatshops, saving the environment, and reforming politics through a more participatory democracy."

Carly Simon

In a book excerpt [The First Day of the Rest of My Life, Newsweek Jan. 22, 2007], Davidson writes that she contacted Carly Simon, "because I'd heard she'd been dealing with multiple blows: she was diagnosed with breast cancer and had a mastectomy at the same time she and her husband were drifting apart, her kids were moving off on their own and her record company was abandoning her."

Simon, she says "felt discarded like a dog... Forced to give up her apartment in Manhattan when the rent was tripled, she moved by herself to Martha's Vineyard where she started recording songs in her daughter's old bedroom. She'd stay up late, mixing tracks on her own, just trying to please herself."

"I was doing what I'd done at 19," Simon said, "making sounds I liked. That was the only star I could follow." She went on to work with producer Richard Perry, with whom she'd made "You're So Vain" and other hits. "He asked her to collaborate on some romantic ballads. They funded the recording themselves and when they were satisfied, sold it to Columbia. The week it was released as 'Moonlight Serenade,' it hit No. 7 on the Billboard chart."

Midlife challenges

There may be substantial personal challenges impacting how we can explore and realize our talents in midlife and later, such as health issues, and re-thinking the skills and values our parents model and teach.

For example, Sally M. Reis, Ph.D. warns in her article "Internal barriers, personal issues, and decisions faced by gifted and talented females" that "The very characteristics found to be associated with older talented women (determination, commitment, assertiveness, and the ability to control their own lives) directly conflict with what some parents encourage as good and appropriate manners in their daughters."

Dr. Reis is author of book Work left undone: Compromises and challenges of talented females.

Ø Ø Ø

> *Emotions*

HAPPINESS - MOOD

"If only we'd stop trying to be happy we could have a pretty good time." – Edith Wharton

"I'm not crazy, I've just been in a very bad mood for 40 years."
Ouiser Boudreaux (Shirley MacLaine), in Steel Magnolias (1989).

In his book <u>The Art of Happiness</u>, The Dalai Lama claims "Whether one believes in religion or not, the very purpose of our life, the very motion of our life is towards happiness."

But many of us aren't so sure about that notion. Of course, the idea of "happiness" is variable; it is not just a simple state of mind or experience that everyone shares or agrees about. I am in general more happy overall than I have been in other phases of my life - part of the advantage of aging, according to some research, but also a matter of not being weighted down with depression. And I certainly am "better" in various ways, at least in part because of positive mood, which may be labeled "happiness."

But what about the effort that Wharton was talking about - the "trying to be happy"? In his review [LA Times Jan 1 2006] of the book <u>Happiness: A History</u> by Darrin M. McMahon, Gordon Marino notes, "As Americans, we have a religious devotion to the idea of our own happiness. We believe that we have a sacred right to pursue that strange bird into the forest of our lives and are even prepared to medicate any condition that gets in the way of the hunt."

That may be the main thing about our personal and cultural obsession: we think it is our right, and can't let anything limit or obscure the condition, and we may pressure ourselves to take immediate steps if we aren't happy "enough."

In his post <u>Is Happiness Overrated?</u>, Professor of Psychology William Todd Schultz, PhD comments, "On one hand, what could anyone want more than happiness? Isn't happiness what we're after?"

But, he continues, "Maybe not. I started mulling this over after reading a New Yorker review of a biography of Koestler [author Arthur Koestler], who was no happiness fan. Nor was Freud, of course, who said the two aims of life were love and work (or, more precisely, sex and ambition)."

Schultz concludes, "I guess my instinct is to say happiness is overrated. I also believe intelligence is overrated, but that's another story. Happiness even gets in the way of success. As poet Philip Larkin once said, 'Happiness writes white.' It takes the lift and the wound out of creative work. One needs the wound. No wound, no high art. Anyway, I couldn't complain about being happy. But I think I'd like to be other things more."

Avoidance is futile

While I do not agree with his idea that "One needs the wound," a strong aversion to emotional and psychic discomfort and avoidance of so-called "negative" feelings in favor of fleeting pleasures that pass for happiness, can inhibit creative vitality.

Robert Epstein, PhD (Editor in Chief of Psychology Today magazine) thinks happiness is "probably not a state we should even try to pursue. It seems to emerge as a byproduct of fulfilling activities."

That idea is also expressed by creativity researcher and psychologist Mihaly Csikszentmihalyi, who thinks "The best moments usually occur when a person's body or mind is stretched to its limits in a voluntary effort to accomplish something difficult and worthwhile." [Quote from my article Creativity and Flow Psychology.]

Csikszentmihalyi is author of "Flow - the Psychology of Optimal Experience" and a number of related books.

The Happiness Trap

In the Introduction to his book The Happiness Trap: How to Stop Struggling, Start Living, Psychotherapist and Executive Coach Russ Harris, MD asks, "What if your very efforts to find happiness were actually preventing you from achieving it?"

He notes "The word 'happiness' has two very different meanings. Usually it refers to a feeling: a sense of pleasure, gladness or gratification…However, like all our other feelings, feelings of happiness don't last…And as we shall see, a life spent in pursuit of those feelings is, in the main, unsatisfying. In fact, the harder we pursue pleasurable feelings, the more we are likely to suffer from anxiety and depression."

He adds, "When we take action on the things that truly matter deep in our hearts, when we move in directions that we consider valuable and worthy, when we clarify what we stand for in life and act accordingly, then our lives become rich and full and meaningful, and we experience a powerful sense of vitality. This is not some fleeting feeling — it is a profound sense of a life well lived. And although such a life will undoubtedly give us many pleasurable feelings, it will also give us uncomfortable ones, such as sadness, fear and anger. This is only to be expected. If we live a full life, we will feel the full range of human emotions."

You can hear a long podcast interview with him at Shrink Rap Radio - an excellent source of interviews with psychologists and others.

Imagination, creativity, happiness

"I don't like emotions... For some reason I'm more comfortable
in imaginary circumstances."
– Actor William H. Macy

One of our primary tools as a creative person is imagination.

But in his book "<u>Stumbling on Happiness</u>" Harvard psychology professor Daniel Gilbert proposes that imagination may directly impact our sense of happiness in limiting or distorting ways.

Meghan Daum writes in her column "Goodbye to you, Mr. Smiley" [Los Angeles Times, May 20, 2006] that the book suggests "happiness is largely an anticipatory experience... we spend much of our time not so much experiencing pleasure as thinking about future pleasure and taking steps to ensure its attainment."

She thinks "the 21st century cultural preoccupation with happiness [is] peer pressure of the most toxic variety... For those whose happiness standards exceed the reach of besotted emoticons, a prescription for a serotonin reuptake inhibitor has become the thinking man's smiley face... But considering the intangible nature of happiness, the inherent ephemeralness of it, the difficulty, even, of defining it, it bears asking why we're so focused on it."

Certainly many creative people do suffer from depression, anxiety and other mood disorders that compromise happiness and impact creative expression, but happiness alone – or even contentment – may not be such a worthwhile goal in itself for a creative person.

I am not suggesting we should not pursue happiness to some extent - and engaging in creative work can be deeply pleasurable and satisfying. But it can be limiting to think happiness is the primary goal.

And reliance on imagination for defining life value can be distorting.

In his review of "Stumbling on Happiness" Malcolm Gladwell [author of Blink: The Power of Thinking Without Thinking] notes that "We're far too accepting of the conclusions of our imaginations. Our imaginations aren't particularly imaginative. Our imaginations are really bad at telling us how we will think when the future finally comes. And our personal experiences aren't nearly as good at correcting these errors as we might think."

Too much positive feeling?

A study by June Gruber of Yale University and others ("A Dark Side of Happiness? How, When, and Why Happiness Is Not Always Good"), notes "Emotional states exert significant effects on memory, judgment, decision-making, and creativity," and reports that "moderate levels of positive emotions engender more creativity, but high levels of positive emotions do not."

The study adds, "Furthermore, when experiencing very high degrees of positive emotion, some individuals are inclined to engage in riskier behaviors, such as alcohol consumption, binge eating, and drug use."

The research is summarized in a press release: Happiness Has a Dark Side.

But happines can help

The above are additional perspectives on our natural pursuit of happiness - I'm not implying happiness or positive psychology efforts are wrong. Feeling good, even happy, is one of the rewards of creative expression.

In the article The 6 Myths Of Creativity (Fast Company magazine, December 1, 2004), psychologist Teresa Amabile (Harvard Business School) reports that her research finds that "people are happiest when they come up with a creative idea, but they're more likely to have a breakthrough if they were happy the day before. There's a kind of virtuous cycle. When people are excited about their work, there's a better chance that they'll make a cognitive association that incubates overnight and shows up as a creative idea the next day. One day's happiness often predicts the next day's creativity."

Watch out for that comfort zone

Keeping ourselves emotionally safe makes sense, of course, but safety and contentment may come at the expense of personal development. I know that has been true for me: I have not pursued some interests or opportunities because of shyness and introversion, for example.

Jack Canfield talks about high achievers being willing to regularly move outside their comfort zone. He also thinks there are important inner aspects of comfort, and says "Unfortunately, many of us have a fairly stubborn tendency to hold on to our old negative thoughts and self images. It's our comfort zone - we've become accustomed to our familiar concepts of reality, and we tend to get stuck in our subconscious beliefs of inadequacy, fear, and doubt." From his article

Who You Are. His book: The Success Principles.

Producer Brian Grazer recalls in his essay "Disrupting My Comfort Zone" about deciding to learn how to surf at age 45. "Picture this scene: The north shore of Oahu—the toughest, most competitive surfing spot on the planet," he writes. "Fourteen-foot swells. Twenty tattooed locals. And me, 5-foot-8-inches of abject terror. What will get me first, I wondered, the next big wave or the guy to my right with the tattoo on his chest that reads 'RIP'? They say that life is tough enough. But I guess I like to make things difficult on myself, because I do that all the time. Every day and on purpose. That's because I believe in disrupting my comfort zone."

Over a career span of over thirty years, he has produced more than fifty movies and twenty television series. "I'm successful and, in my business, pretty well known. I'm a guy who could retire to the golf course tomorrow where the worst that could happen is that my Bloody Mary is watered-down. So why do I continue to subject myself to this sort of thing? The answer is simple: Disrupting my comfort zone, bombarding myself with challenging people and situations — this is the best way I know to keep growing. And to paraphrase a biologist I once met, if you're not growing, you're dying."

The article "Disrupting My Comfort Zone" by Brian Grazer is on the site thisibelieve.org, and in the book <u>This I Believe</u>.

An additional perspective is provided by personal achievement author and coach Brian Tracy in his article <u>The Indispensable Quality</u>. "Most people are seduced by the lure of the comfort zone," he writes. "This can be likened to going out of a warm house on a cold, windy morning. The average person, when he feels the storm swirling outside his comfort zone, rushes back inside where it's nice and warm. But not the true leader. The true leader has the courage to step away from the familiar and comfortable and to face the unknown with no guarantees of success. It is this ability to 'boldly go where no man has gone before' that distinguishes you as a leader from the average person."

[Also see Brian Tracy's titles on the development of human potential and personal effectiveness at <u>Nightingale-Conant</u>.]

Stretching beyond our comfort level

A number of actors say they consciously avoid a comfort zone in considering scripts, and performing. Sandra Bullock says, "I don't do anything anymore that feels safe. If it doesn't scare the crap out of you, then you're

not doing the right thing." From my post
<u>Developing creativity: Fear is not a disease</u>.

Of course fear - one of the prime
feelings we may experience when moving
beyond our comfort zone - can be self-
protective, and indicate real danger. At least
sometimes. The problem is, we can feel fear
when it is in our best interest to go ahead and
do something anyway.

Writer Chris Green comments in his
article <u>The Thief of Fulfilment</u>, "As soon as you
start to consider making changes to your life,
your subconscious mind will play the fear card.
You are leaving the comfort zone and boy-oh-
boy, does it not like it! Not one little bit!" He
adds, "This is no joke. It happens to millions of
people and this fear ruins their dreams for a
better life. And here's the danger of giving in to
this fear: You can feel as though you're stuck in
a rut – kind of like life is passing you by."

So maybe people of courage like those
actors and producer Brian Grazer are on to
something that can help any of us lead a
bigger life.

Naomi Judd points out in her book
<u>Naomi's Breakthrough Guide: 20 Choices to
Transform Your Life</u>, "Risk taking is a funny
thing. Each time you risk, it becomes easier to
do. That's because each time you go for it, it
further reinforces your self-esteem and offers

concrete evidence that you can indeed succeed."

Embracing discomfort to grow and achieve

There are many different kinds of discomfort in addition to fear and mood disorders like anxiety, some mild, some requiring change, even intervention or therapy, or at least greater self-care.

In her article Discovering the Gifted Ex-Child, Stephanie S. Tolan writes about one highly talented person with the discomfort of stage fright. "Barbra Streisand, whose abilities are not only obvious and far from norms but also wide-ranging, is criticized for perfectionism, for demanding too much from those she works with. Her well-known discomfort with public performance may come in part from the seemingly paradoxical self-esteem problems that often come with extraordinary gifts."

Discomfort, of course, can also be an indicator that something is "off" or even potentially harmful in your body, or in a relationship or other parts of your life. But it may also be just part of your experience at the growing edge toward being more and doing more - creatively and in other areas.

Therapist and writer Nathaniel Branden has commented, "Innovators and creators are persons who can to a higher degree than average accept the condition of aloneness. They are more willing to follow their own vision, even when it takes them far from the mainland of the human community. Unexplored places do not frighten them – or not, at any rate, as much as they frighten those around them. This is one of the secrets of their power. That which we call 'genius' has a great deal to do with courage and daring, a great deal to do with nerve."

See one of Nathaniel Branden's books: 6 Pillars of Self Esteem, and his program The Psychology of High Self-Esteem.

Adept at taking risks

Kim Yasuda, co-director of the UC Institute for Research in the Arts, at UC Santa Barbara, also thinks "Artists are remarkably adept at taking risks, at negotiating the terrain of uncertainty. Qualities of resourcefulness and fluidity are necessary to remain an innovator in today's cultural climate." [93106 news magazine of UCSB, April 4 2005]

Humanistic psychologist Abraham Maslow (1908-1970) declared, "One can choose to go back toward safety or forward toward growth. Growth must be chosen again and again; fear must be overcome again and again."

Being seduced by the comfort of routine and the known

Even though our routines may be useful and productive, some of them can be self-limiting, especially if we keep following them without awareness.

In his book on personal development and achievement, Unhypnosis, Steve Taubman writes that some people experience "atrophy of imagination" from a "continued repetition of an unsatisfactory life script."

Master Designer Susan Kirkland notes in her post Surviving Troublemakers, "Idealism and youth perpetuate risk and adventure. As time passes, wisdom may view risk with trepidation, shelving adventure in favor of security. Choosing the predictable over the unknown buys us comfort and sadly, mediocrity."

Hopefully, becoming more aware of the ruts we make for ourselves can help us live more fully and creatively.

Ø Ø Ø

INSPIRATION - PASSION

One of the most widely circulated quotes on passion and personal development is this one by author and mythologist Joseph Campbell: "When you follow your bliss... doors will open where you would not have thought there would be doors; and where there wouldn't be a door for anyone else."

That may be a bit new-agey for my taste, but I still like it, especially if I interpret "doors" as inner perception, rather than simply external opportunities.

Campbell also said, "To find your own way is to follow your bliss. This involves analysis, watching yourself and seeing where real deep bliss is -- not the quick little excitement, but the real deep, life-filling bliss."

That can be a life-long exploration, of course - especially for multitalented people - and your 'blisses' may change over time, even radically - including your vocational interests. See the chapter on Work - Career and Barbara Sher's ideas on being a Scanner. Reading about people with passionate serial interests - 'Scanners' - who may not fit into mainstream occupational roles has been very enlightening and affirming for me; one form of criticizing myself has been to wonder if I'm too 'crazy' to stick with an interest or job, then feel shame because so many people, even exceptional ones, do seem able to find and pursue a 'niche' in life.

Michelangelo as a role model

"Many people die with their music still in them. Why is this so? Too often it is because they are always getting ready to live. Before they know it, time runs out." – Oliver Wendell Holmes

The book The Michelangelo Method promises to use the Italian Renaissance painter, sculptor, architect, poet and engineer as a model for gaining insight into our own creative life, and releasing our music – our potential talents.

Here is a section from the book that talks about some of the feelings we may experience - such as regret - over not realizing our talents, and how we may think of our talents or gifts. It's a long excerpt, because I think it refers to a number of important topics, such as identifying ourselves as gifted or exceptional.

"Susan worked as a legal assistant for a major law firm. Her daughter, 'the flower from my compost heap of a marriage' as she put it, had recently left for college on an academic scholarship. With her daughter launched, Susan was left to consider her own path. She looked down at the ground below her. 'Dull cement,' she said, 'and my feet were planted in it long before I had a chance to choose.' Susan wanted a change. She was dying for a change. But to what? She had no idea. And wasn't it too late already? After all, she was nearly 42.

"Susan couldn't think constructively. She believed that she had no choices. Here was a bright, articulate, capable woman who, in her own mind, could never do anything right and believed she had missed her chance anyway. Susan thought her life nothing more than a giant 'might have been.' If she hadn't married so young, she might have had a relationship she was happy with. If she hadn't gotten pregnant, she might have finished law school. If she had finished law school, she could have been the lawyer and not the legal assistant."

The book continues, "Susan couldn't figure out where to begin. Her early enchantment with the law had faded. She wanted a new life, and her greatest fear was, to paraphrase Oliver Wendell Holmes, that she might die with her music still in her. For Susan, it was time to start playing her own music. Working with a life coach, Susan asked, 'How do I find out what exactly to do? Can you tell me?' 'You have to find it within yourself,' the coach said. 'But I can start by asking you a few questions that will begin to reveal your gift.'

"'But I don't have a particular gift. I'm not gifted,' Susan said. "If you were to ask someone what their gift is, chances are their minds will immediately turn to Michelangelo sculpting his Pietà or Einstein unlocking the universe's secrets with a simple equation. People tend to think of gifts in such extraordinary terms. They see a gift as an innate, exceptional talent, as something that few people in this life are born with. But they are wrong.

"A gift isn't just the province of the exceptionally talented, the successful, or the blessed. Quite the contrary, everyone has a gift. Some gifts are thousand-watt bolts of light. Others are hidden in the stone. All are there, waiting to be revealed. Your gift lies in the place where your values, passions, and strengths meet. Discovering that place is the first step toward sculpting your masterpiece, your life."

Excerpt from "Finding Your Gift" By Ken Schuman and Ron Paxton (posted on Oprah.com) – from the book The Michelangelo Method.

Developing creativity with passion

Challenge may be an important part of creative expression and developing talents, and passion is part of the intrinsic motivation that keeps creators going in the face of challenges.

In an article of hers ("Hollywood is Hard"), actor Amber Tamblyn cautions that you need to find and use your passion, especially with all the rejection and uncertainty of acting - which can happen, of course, in other creative fields.

"A lot of people think I'm cynical when I talk about acting," she writes. "The truth of the matter is, I just don't want someone to get some lame advice that will send them in the wrong direction. I want people to find their true love in working, whether it be acting, teaching, or any other job. Bottom line: Be Careful! A business like acting is 90% luck. You can be a star one minute and out of work the next. Always keep your hopes high and your energy positive, and don't think it's impossible, but know that it's very hard."

Following your creative inspiration in spite of difficulties.

Actor Elisha Cuthbert commented about moving from Montreal to L.A. at age 17 to pursue acting: "I just went with my gut feeling and thought that if I care this much about what I'm doing, then maybe there are opportunities elsewhere and I'd be stupid not to give it a try." [imdb.com bio]

Working with Jodie Foster in their movie "Contact," Jena Malone, then about age 12, recalled in our interview about Foster giving her advice that works for any artist: "Sometimes I did things that I didn't all the way want to do. I half way wanted to do them, or something like that, and I always regretted it. So, I want you to always follow your heart and do exactly what you always wished for. You're only going to be happy when you follow your heart."

Happiness and other positive feelings can be a significant part of this talent exploration journey - and something I write more about in the previous chapter.

Filmmaker George Lucas declares "You have to find something that you love enough to be able to take risks, jump over the hurdles and break through the brick walls that are always going to be placed in front of you. If you don't have that kind of feeling for what it is you are doing, you'll stop at the first giant hurdle." [Quoted in a newsletter of Bob Proctor.]

But Stephen Gaghan, screenwriter of "Traffic," "Syriana" and other films, has commented that many creative people in the entertainment field are not able – or willing – to follow their real passions: "It's rare in Hollywood to get the chance to work on something that you actually care about. The tragedy of the place is all these talented people trying to get excited about stuff they themselves would only view at gunpoint." [Quote from imdb.com]

Painter Amanda Dunbar, acclaimed in her teens as a prodigy, commented in our interview: "As artists, we use not only our technical abilities to execute our work, but also all of our mental capacities, our spirituality, and at the same time we must make that leap of faith (that we all struggle to articulate) every time we begin our work. Some would consider this 'irrational'. Why put yourself through all that agony for something that may or may not 'pay off' at the end? In my opinion, the answer is that it satisfies that innate and unexplainable yet powerful drive to create."

That drive can strongly impact how a creative person interacts with others. Kate Winslet's director for their film "The Holiday," Nancy Meyers, commented about Winslet's appeal and passion: "People do love her. The only other person I've ever seen love acting that much is Jack Nicholson." [From article

What Kate Winslet Knows, by Karen Valby,
Entertainment Weekly, Oct 6 2006.]

Psychiatrist Kay Redfield Jamison talks
about passion in terms of enthusiasm. Author
of Touched with Fire: Manic-Depressive Illness
and the Artistic Temperament, in her newer
book Exuberance : The Passion for Life, she
wants people to "appreciate how life-saving
exuberance is to us as a species. I have
always been fascinated by mania. There is an
exhilaration in the early stages of mania that
people who have experienced it would sell their
firstborn to feel again. Mania is a sickness; it's
easy to romanticize unless you've been there."

Jamison continued, "What is really
healthy and great is exuberance. A passion for
life, an exuberant temperament, allows people
to do things they wouldn't be able to do if they
didn't have it."

Mania can have a huge impact on
personal achievement and creative expression,
and many prominent business pioneers and
artists have experienced bipolar disorder or the
related hypomania. For more on this topic, see
the TalentDevelop page: hypomania.

Creative passion and inspiration can get deflated or displaced.

In the movie "Adaptation" (based on the book The Orchid Thief, by Susan Orlean, with screenplay by Charlie Kaufman about his own struggles as a writer), the character Charlie Kaufman [Nicolas Cage] sits at his typewriter: "To begin...To begin...How to start? I'm hungry. I should get coffee. Coffee would help me think. Maybe I should write something first, then reward myself with coffee. Coffee and a muffin. So I need to establish the themes. Maybe a banana nut. That's a good muffin."

Does that sound at all familiar? It certainly is for me.

Orlean has an insightful perspective in her book: "I was starting to believe that the reason it matters to care passionately about something is that it whittles the world down to a more manageable size. It makes the world seem not huge and empty but full of possibility."

But pursuing our passions is not necessarily a simple or easy matter, as actor Alice Krige has noted: "It seems to me that the greatest challenge, at once the easiest and the hardest thing for human beings to do, is to follow our passion."

[Quotes from the TalentDevelop page: passion]

And it isn't always easy or natural for many high ability people to acknowledge the value of the good achievements our passions lead to. One reason may be that some people hold a stereotyped view of what giftedness or exceptional talent means (as merely high IQ, for example) and feel that an identity as "gifted" is incompatible with their self-concept.

Others may have a fear of failure or success related to living up to the label, or have an aversion to being thought "elitist", "superior", or "hogging all the glory" — and they may feel guilt, shame, or other destabilizing feelings about being exceptional.

Highly talented women, according to some research, may hide abilities in order to survive socially.

M. Scott Peck noted in his book "The Road Less Traveled and Beyond" [quoted in my article Gifted Women: Identity and Expression], that "Many who are truly superior...are reluctant to consider themselves 'better than' or 'above' others, in large part because a sense of humility accompanies their personal and spiritual power."

As I noted earlier, one of the values of the book "Enjoying the Gift of Being Uncommon" by Willem Kuipers is the author's use of a different framing of exceptional ability as Xi: eXtra intelligent or eXtra intense.

Living your passion

In an interview with Alex Mandossian by Patrick Coffey & Chris Attwood, they quote the Indian sage Patanjali: "When you are inspired by some great purpose, some extraordinary project, all your thoughts break their bonds. Your mind transcends limitations, your consciousness expands in every direction, and you find yourself in a new, great and wonderful world. Dormant forces, faculties and talents become alive and you discover yourself to be a greater person by far than you ever dreamed yourself to be."

Alex Mandossian (an online marketing expert, speaker and author) comments that during an earlier period of his life, he was a workaholic: "I was working 16 hours a day. I don't know if you are familiar with New York City, but if you come home before 9:00 PM at night, you are not working hard enough. People come back to their apartments and to their studios and one bedroom, two bedroom apartments in three piece suits at 9:00 – 10:00 o'clock at night. That is normal. That is just the way life is in Manhattan...I didn't realize back then that there was a collision between personal and professional passion." From interview: Choices: When Passions Collide.

There may also be a collision or conflict between your passions and your health.

Using movies to explore passions and interests

Films may be primarily designed to entertain, but a number of writers and psychologists point out that movies can illuminate ways we may grow and realize creative talents, or point out ways we get blocked.

In an article of hers, Maria Grace, PhD offers an exercise in using films: "The characters in the following films are different but they all share one characteristic in common: their lives are determined by their willingness to be creative. They can inspire you to trust your creativity and follow your creative impulses until they bring fruits in your life. Choose a film and watch it alone or with a group of friends. Answer the questions at the end of the list in writing and discuss your answers with your friends. Repeat the same with more films...

• Amadeus (1984)
• Artemisia (1997)
• Chocolat (2000)
• Frida (2002)
• Music of the Heart (1999)
• Shall We Dance? (2004)

Questions to answer:
1. What role does creativity play in the life of the main character of the story?
2. How does the environment respond to the main character's creativity?
3. What forces in the character's life do oppose his/her creativity? Notice that these forces may be not only external, but also internal."

[Continued in article <u>How to Become Creative with Inspiration from Movies</u>,]

Make your own movie

Many personal development experts such as Bob Proctor support the use of visualization as a strategy for life change. One powerful method to make use of visualization is to create your own mini-movie with images, text and sounds that have meaning for you. A very popular software program for doing this is <u>Mind Movies</u>.

Following up

"When you're passionate, you may not be good at what you're doing in the beginning. But if you have to do it to follow your passions, then experience will make you good at it."

From the site of The Passion Test. You can take a free profile on the site.

Of course, it takes more than simply feeling passionate about something. The elements of experience, focus and persistence are also crucial. But many people may find the advice to "Find your passion" to be useless or even fearful.

Author Daniel Pink (A Whole New Mind: Why Right-Brainers Will Rule the Future) has said, "I find that question very daunting. What's your passion? I find that almost paralyzing, in a way. I find it less paralyzing to say, What are you interested in doing next?"

I like his idea. Sometimes the concept of 'passion' seems so large and indelible it can be stifling. On the other hand, really thinking about what to do next in your life may not be a small or trivial question, but is likely to be something we can more readily do.

Underestimating and undervaluing

Personal development expert Earl Nightingale notes in his article The Great Problem-Solving Tool that "Each of us has a tendency to underestimate his or her own abilities. We should realize that we have deep within ourselves deep reservoirs of great ability, even genius that can be tapped if we'll just dig deep enough."

But it can be difficult for many people to uncover and encourage their multiple talents and creative abilities.

Career and creativity writer Gail McMeekin comments in her article <u>Creative Catalysts</u>, "We are all originals and have the software to be creative. Yet, sometimes we feel blocked or uninspired and can't get our creativity to click."

She suggests a number of simple strategies to try, including:

* Keep a daily excitement list about WHY you are passionate and committed to your exploration or project.

* Change your location – work on your project in bed, outside in nature, in a coffee shop, or a different room; Take a trip relating to your project to explore a facet of it.

* Go to a toy store and find a toy like your project and play with it.

* Set up a series of experiments related to your project

With a bit of creative thought, you can expand those ideas to stimulate a more profound exploration of your abilities and interests.

Religion and faith often fuel creative expression

Various religious traditions have inspired and financially supported artists probably for as long as humanity has had religion. Religious belief and passion fuel much of art and literature - and can be another window on your creative talents.

For example, there is now a series of films based on the books The Chronicles of Narnia by C. S. Lewis.

Another example is Anne Rice, who grew up in New Orleans a Catholic, but abandoned it at 18 to live in the Haight-Ashbury and write her vampire Lestat series. She also wrote pornography and erotica under pen names.

About her life in the late 1950s she says, "I felt I had to deal with my faith and reconcile it with the world around me. My childhood was very sex-obsessed and repressed. I felt when I accepted a world without God, I accepted reality, and stopped believing in illusion."

Following the death of her husband in 2002, she returned to her faith in a new way, realizing "I didn't have to write the books I had been writing forever." One of her novels is on the boyhood of Jesus: "Christ the Lord: Out of Egypt." Rice has commented, "I think it's sad that the strident voices of Christianity have cemented in the public mind that we are dumb. I feel I have to play my role as an artist and creator. But like many Christians, I want to speak out for what I believe in." [Quotes from Twists of faith, By Anne-Marie O'Connor, Los Angeles Times Dec 26, 2005.]

Spirituality

"The creative process shrivels in the absence of continual dialogue with the soul. And creativity is what makes life worth living."

That is a quote by Jungian analyst and author Marion Woodman, on a topic also addressed by Julia Cameron in her classic book The Artist's Way: A Spiritual Path to Higher Creativity. Cameron writes, "The heart of creativity is an experience of the mystical union... Those who speak in spiritual terms routinely refer to God as the creator but seldom see 'creator' as the literal term for 'artist.' I am suggesting you take the term creator quite literally. You are seeking to forge a creative alliance, artist to artist, with the Great Creator."

Whether you think of this "Great Creator" as a deity or "higher power" or "Gaia" or something else, there is a powerful element of inspiration from spiritual awareness and sensibility that complements the intellectual aspects of creative work.

Another writer on this subject is Canadian philosopher Charles Taylor, who won the 2007 Templeton Prize for Progress Toward Research or Discoveries About Spiritual Realities. A newspaper article reported that Taylor said the prevailing emphasis on the secular in the contemporary culture of science and academic study had shortchanged humanity. It is impossible, he said, to "really understand" what makes people and societies "tick" without considering both the secular and spiritual.

"People must be able to think in both languages, in both levels — not just with one half of their brain," Taylor said. To leave out the spiritual is like "working with the other half [of the brain] frozen." In his statement on the Templeton Prize site, Taylor writes that "a blindness to the spiritual dimension of human life makes us incapable of exploring issues which are vital to our lives. Or to turn it around and state the positive: bringing the spiritual back in opens domains in which important and even exciting discoveries become possible." [Los Angeles Times, March 15, 2007.]

Have you found there is a spiritual dimension to your creative expression?

Ø Ø Ø

COURAGE - FEAR - ANXIETY

Many of the personal, inner aspects of creative talent can challenge us in ways that demand facing fears and limitations and moving beyond our comfort zones. And many forms of creative expression may require at times a high degree of courage. I have certainly had to summon courage for some actions - and have avoided others out of insufficient passion or clarity or courage.

What have others noted about all this?

In an HBO documentary about making movies, actor Charlize Theron commented about courage when she noted, "There is no formula that works. There is no guarantee. But as far as making choices on material, I just kind of think, well, it has nothing to do with me, so why not just go for it? That's why, when people say, Why don't you make safer choices,

I say What is a safe choice? There really isn't a safe choice in this industry. You never have a guarantee whether it's going to work or not. And it takes a lot of courage to do that. So you better make sure, if it doesn't work, that you walk away with something else, and that is the knowledge that you did it for a good reason."

[From HBO documentary Boffo! Tinseltown's Bombs and Blockbusters, June 2006, based on the book Boffo! : How I Learned to Love the Blockbuster and Fear the Bomb, by Peter Bart.

The condition of aloneness

Writer and therapist Nathaniel Branden (well-known for his writing and counseling on self-esteem issues) notes about the courage aspect of making creative choices: "Innovators and creators are persons who can to a higher degree than average accept the condition of aloneness. They are more willing to follow their own vision, even when it takes them far from the mainland of the human community. This is one of the secrets of their power. That which we call 'genius' has a great deal to do with courage and daring, a great deal to do with nerve."

[One of his books is The Art of Living Consciously]

French philosopher Simone Weil noted, "The human soul has need of security and also of risk. The boredom produced by a complete absence of risk is also a sickness of the soul."

But risking with too much abandon, too little rational concern or awareness, can be futile or even self-destructive. Artists and other people who learn to walk that edge are the ones who succeed in creative projects and other endeavors.

Playing too small – are you holding back your creative potential?

T. Harv Eker, founder and president of personal development company Peak Potentials Training, comments about self-limiting fear in his book Secrets of the Millionaire Mind. and training program The Millionaire Mind Intensive.

"What I have witnessed is too many people playing far too small, and too many people allowing their fear-based ego selves to rule them," he says. "The result is that too many of us are not living up to our full potential, in terms of both our own lives and our contribution to others. Your life is not just about you. It's also about contributing to others. It's about living true to your mission and reason for being here on this earth at this time."

Eker quotes the well-known passage by Marianne Williamson from her book A Return To Love: "You are a child of God. Your playing small doesn't serve the world. There's nothing enlightened about shrinking so that other people won't feel insecure around you. We are all meant to shine, as children do. We were born to manifest the glory of God that is within us. It's not just in some of us; it's in everyone. And as we let our own light shine, we unconsciously give other people permission to do the same. As we're liberated from our own fear, our presence automatically liberates others."

Even if you don't have or agree with a particular concept of God, there is something very powerful about the idea of "letting our own light shine" and releasing our creative abilities by not holding back.

In his book Secrets of the Millionaire Mind, Eker talks about the value of living with distress and discomfort, and using it positively: "The first time you tried something new, was it comfortable or uncomfortable?" he writes. "Usually uncomfortable. But what happened afterword? The more you did it, the more comfortable it became, right? That's how it goes.. if you stick with it and continue, you will eventually move through the uncomfort zone and succeed."

An additional value is that you will have "a new, expanded comfort zone, which means you will have become a 'bigger' person. The only time you are actually growing is when you are uncomfortable."

Growing beyond discomfort

Experiences that many talented people may have that can keep them (us) "playing small" include introversion, unhealthy self-esteem and anxiety, such as fear of public speaking. All of which can be faced and improved or even overcome so our talents can be more fully expressed – and have a greater positive impact on other people.

Many, if not all, kinds of anxiety may be affected by our beliefs and thinking, as well as our physiology.

In his article <u>The fear will go away if I practice enough</u>, Morty Lefkoe notes, "You can speak in public without fear. But you cannot do it with the beliefs you currently hold, whatever they may be. The way you look at people, at your performance in public, and at yourself must change in order for your fears to go away."

Lefkoe has developed a number of programs to change self-limiting beliefs, acclaimed by Jack Canfield among many others. Two of those programs are Undo Public Speaking Fear and ReCreate Your Life - where you can eliminate a limiting belief free.

In her article Preparing For Performance, Linda Dessau writes about stage fright and anxiety that can "keep artists locked away in their own homes, carefully guarding their creative gifts. Then those gifts never see the light of day, and they're never seen by the world.

She writes, "For some of us, simply facing our art form and giving voice to our creativity is a performance. For others, it might be meeting with an art gallery owner, a submission to a contest, fulfilling a commissioned piece of artwork for a customer or something else that brings up similar fears and self-doubt."

Being an entrepreneur

One arena in which talented people can make use of their creative abilities is business - especially small business and self-employment.

Even if they don't necessarily think of themselves that way, artists are entrepreneurs. Elia Woods, an Oklahoma City artist, has worked with Alyson B. Stanfield, an art business consultant for artists, galleries, and organizations.

Woods commented, "As an artist, my weak areas were marketing and the business aspect of selling my artwork. I have put a lot of energy into learning my artistic skills but not a lot into the business side." Woods said working with Stanfield was worth the time and effort away from creating, because it helped get her work into local and national exhibits.

From article: "Web site helps artists develop business plan" by Tricia Pemberton, The Oklahoman - available at Stanfield's site Art Biz Coach.

Other resources include The Right-Brain Business Plan book and various programs by coach, writer and artist Jennifer Lee, available at her site Artizen Coaching.

Tom Peters on being creative in business

In his article The Entrepreneurial Spirit, management expert Tom Peters asks, "Feeling a little weird lately? Take time to see where your passion and entrepreneurial spirit is calling you. Even in corporate America, the entrepreneurial spirit must remain alive. That spirit can solve the toughest of corporate problems, if only we let it."

See Tom Peters books and programs, plus many other business and personal development authors, at YourSuccessStore and at Nightingale-Conant.

Also see more articles for entrepreneurs, and my site The Inner Entrepreneur, and related Facebook page The Inner Entrepreneur.

Farrah Gray is an example of achievement as an entrepreneur. He grew up near the East Chicago housing projects, where he found that "Selling drugs is real easy. You benefit on the front end and pay like hell on the back end. My attitude is I work hard on the front end so I can benefit on the back end." He explains, "I realized very very very very early that the same knowledge it would take me to buy, wholesale, and sell I could take that same knowledge as opposed to selling drugs. I think selling drugs is a weak way out."

Gray has always had an insatiable drive to succeed, which stems from his life filled with struggle. At age eight, he formed Urban Neighborhood Economic Enterprise Club, that encouraged youth to become entrepreneurs. Before the age of 19, Gray had acquired Innercity Magazine and signed a deal for his book Reallionaire: Nine Steps to Becoming Rich from the Inside Out. Now that Gray is a millionaire, he advises others through his book and presentations.

"The biggest mistake I made was believing that someone was gonna do something for me." He has also found that you should "Never fear rejection. The wounded deer is the one who leaps the highest. In life we don't get what we want, we get in life what we are. If we want more we have to be able to be more, in order to be more you have to face rejection." [From blackcollegeview.com February 17, 2005.]

Conditioning and mediocrity

One of the challenges many of us have had to face as multitalented people is to face the consequences (such as social reactions) of being uncommon. We also need to honor our discomfort with mediocrity - in others and ourselves.

According to a news story about the making of the movie "A Prairie Home Companion," director Robert Altman used the phrase "That was adequate" to indicate he had shot enough takes of a scene. One of the stars of the film, Virginia Madsen, said when he tells an actor their performance is "more than adequate, that means it's good."

Garrison Keillor further explained, "It's that Midwestern reticence," noting that Altman grew up in Kansas City, Mo. "The distrust of superlatives is rather strong." [St. Paul Pioneer Press July 20, 2005]

Using that sort of muting of "excessive" enthusiasm for comic effect is one of the pleasures of Keillor's radio show – but in "real" life it may be a form of conditioning toward suppression of passions which can energize our talents.

Columbia Business School Professor Srikumar Rao, in his book <u>Are You Ready to Succeed?</u>, details some of the forms of conditioning we can be subjected to that limit us. He asks, "Are you beset by fears? Are you terrified of spiders or snakes or one-eyed albino pirates? Do dark spaces or soaring heights make your palms sweat? Or does the thought of going to parties, giving speeches, making presentations, or speaking up for something you believe in that is unpopular scare you silly? Are you numbed by the specter of being stuck in the same dreary career and never achieving the potential you know you have? I regularly hear about all these and many, many more. But where did you pick this up? These fears are all a result of your conditioning… from your parents and teachers and role models.. the media that surrounds you."

He adds, "Marketers call it cultural conditioning – your tendency to consume products and think in ways that conform to the broader society that you are a part of. This conditioning not only restricts you, it also prevents you from exploring pathways that could lead you to freedom. That is why you feel boxed in and enervated."

Talented and insecure – gifted adults & low self esteem

Over the years of reading biographies and interviews with many highly talented and creative people, it has often struck me how many of them talk about being self-critical and having poor self-esteem.

For example, writer Larry Kane commented about his bio on the musician, "People would be surprised at how insecure John Lennon was, and his lack of self esteem. Throughout his life, even during the height of Beatle mania, he had poor self esteem, even though he exuded confidence."

Lennon reportedly said about his conflicted feelings, "I'm not going to change the way I look or the way I feel to conform to anything. I've always been a freak...all my life and I have to live with that, you know…Part of me suspects that I'm a loser, and the other part of me thinks I'm God Almighty…You're just left with yourself all the time, whatever you do anyway." [From brainyquote.com]

Self esteem is basically positive self-regard, a realistic acknowledgment of our talents and value as a person. It is not the absurd and trivializing efforts over recent years to make all children in school feel they are "special" and have high [often meaning bloated] self-esteem, as in: "We don't want anyone to feel left out, so everyone wins a spelling bee award" or "The valedictorian will be chosen by lottery."

Continued in my Creative Mind post Creative But Insecure.

I am mentioning this topic here, because it seems to me it can relate to having limitations of courage or not being able to deal adequately with fear.

Many actors and other performers, for example, have reported that, over time, they increased their level of self-esteem through going on stage in spite of fear.

Patti Smith on learning and growing

Patti Smith was called the "high priestess of punk" in the 70s, but in an interview she admits, "I didn't feel that I was growing as an artist at that point. All of my energy was being put into peripheral things – interviews and getting my picture taken. Constantly. And concerts and touring and every minute going to radio stations. In the end I wasn't growing, so the things that I had to talk about… I just didn't know about life. And I thought, I haven't done anything to merit this kind of attention."

She made the choice to spend the '80s "learning quite a bit about our world, about our political situation, about sports, learning how to be a citizen, learning to cook, learning how to sew hems on my kids' uniforms, learning how to nurse children, learning how to scrub diapers and a toilet."

She notes there is "a lot to learn and I was, for a short period of time, living a very sheltered, privileged position for doing very little; for singing rock'n'roll songs. And I felt that I had to reassess that."

She advises others to "kick doors open yourself. When people come up to me and say, 'Patti, nobody wants to hear my CD and I don't have enough money for equipment,' I say, 'Well, get a job, y'know?' That's what I did. You get people who say, 'The government won't give me a grant and I can't do my art.' I say, 'F*** you, it's your own fault, you expect the government to give you a hand? The government is corrupt. Do what it takes. You do babysitting jobs, you work in the factory, you work in the bookstore or become a pickpocket, y'know? But whatever. Get a job.' Work is really good for an artist." [From interview article by Laura Barton, The Guardian, Jan 19, 2007.]

Biography: Patti Smith: American Artist. Her book of poetry: Auguries of Innocence.

Judy and Hilary Swank on courage

Exploring who we are, putting ourselves into places and situations that develop our talents and abilities, standing up to internal and external pressures that get in the way – all that takes courage, and dealing with fear in positive ways.

After being fired from her office job of nine years, Judy Swank initially felt despair at being able to continue supporting her daughter Hilary in her dream to be an actor, but decided to move to California, as she describes in her HuffingtonPost entry Journey Down the Road. "Our grand adventure to Hollywood was the first time that I did the unexpected," Judy Swank writes. "The first time I really took a risk. I had no money and could certainly be thought of as either extremely naïve or just plain crazy.

But whatever was ahead of us, I knew we would figure it out.

She says she did not come to this conclusion on her own: "I gained this knowledge by watching my daughter. The most revealing thing I discovered was how much courage Hilary has. Some times when the door of opportunity opens, we spend too much time deliberating on whether to go through the door or not, all the while the door is slowly closing. Hilary's youth and complete exuberance for what she'd chosen in life allowed her to be unafraid to take the risks involved in pursuing her dream… She followed her instincts. I had learned to believe in them. I completely believed in her."

Hilary Swank said about her powerful role in "Boys Don't Cry": "I wanted to play the joy of living your life the way you want to. It's a beautiful love story. And I think people are reacting to the fact that this was a person who had the courage to live life the way he wanted to. I think everyone wishes they could do that." [Interview mag., April, 2000.]

She has also commented on trying to achieve your goals: "As in life, your mind can be the hugest obstacle or tool, depending on how you choose to use it. And I find that a lot of people who are successful in life say, 'I can do this, and I will do this.' Their minds don't get in their way; whereas people who wake up and say, 'Oh, I can't,' their mind is in their way, and it's going to stop them from doing what they need to do to achieve their dream." [imdb.com]

We all have fears

As Arianna Huffington points out, "Fear is universal; we all have fear." But, she adds in her book <u>On Becoming Fearless</u>, that some fears "do tend to be more prevalent among women than men, including fear of staying single; fear of imperfection; fear of failure; of ugliness; of loneliness; of growing old; public speaking; ridicule; being alone; getting wrinkles."

Those kinds of fears - many of which also affect us men - can hold us back from realizing our talents as fully as we could. And there are many other varieties; it's worth really looking at the fears and anxieties you have. To repeat Professor Srikumar Rao's question from above: "Are you terrified of spiders or snakes or one-eyed albino pirates? Do dark spaces or soaring heights make your palms sweat? Or does the thought of going to parties, giving speeches, making presentations, or speaking up for something you believe in that is unpopular scare you silly?"

Those are likely descriptions of phobias, stage fright, social anxiety or other forms of anxiety - not simply fear. Fortunately, anxiety can be overcome.

My motivation for developing my Anxiety Relief Solutions site was to research ways to help relieve my own anxiety, and to provide information on natural, herbal and self-help products and programs that would benefit other people.

We need high energy – not anxiety – for creative work

There seems to be an enduring mythology about some kinds of creative inspiration and work - performing as an actor, for example - that it benefits from an "edge" of nervous tension or even anxiety.

Creativity coach, psychologist and writer Eric Maisel, PhD comments in our interview Ten Zen Seconds (about his book) that this really is a false and distorting idea: "It isn't at all clear that tension or anxiety is what's needed for peak performance and lifelong creativity."

He says stress and even anxiety "may be unavoidable by-products of the difficulties that we face as we try to do large things and connected to our fear of failing, fear of making messes and mistakes, and so on, but they are not beneficial per se. You want enthusiasm, passion, love, curiosity, interest, and so on to inform your work and to exist right in the moment, in the performance moment or the creative moment, while at the same reducing (or eliminating) your fears, worries, anxieties, and so on."

He notes, "Creating is not an energy-neutral state: it is a high energy state, with, at its healthiest, enthusiasm and not anxiety driving its engine." In his book Mastering Creative Anxiety, Maisel points out how much an impact anxiety may have for creators.

"Are you creating less often than you would like? Are you avoiding your creative work altogether? If so, anxiety may be the culprit! Anxiety regularly stops creative people in their tracks and makes their experience of creating more painful than pleasurable."

In twenty-four lessons in the book, he describes "many of the sources of anxiety in a creative person's life and provide you with an anxiety mastery menu of strategies and techniques."

Resources:

Anxiety articles

Depression and Creativity site

Ø Ø Ø

> *Interacting*

ENVIRONMENT

One basic way that environment impacts creative potential and expression is in terms of the places we choose to live and work. I have certainly noticed at times how much a particular apartment, and neighborhood - even the "tone" of a city - has affected my motivation and energy.

In 1946, George Orwell, although he was very ill, chose to write "Nineteen Eighty-Four" while living in Barnhill, a remote farmhouse on the isle of Jura in the Inner Hebrides. Following the success of his novel Animal Farm, he told his friend Arthur Koestler, "Everyone keeps coming at me, wanting me to lecture, to write commissioned booklets, to join this and that, etc - you don't know how I pine to be free of it all and have time to think again." [From The masterpiece that killed

George Orwell, by Robert McCrum, The Observer, 10 May 2009.]

Many people have talked about the importance of place, work space and solitude for developing creative talents.

In her essay A Room of One's Own in 1929, Virginia Woolf said that for women artists "a lock on the door means the power to think for oneself" and encouragement to develop the "habit of freedom and the courage to write exactly what we think."

Marylou Kelly Streznewski is author of the book "Gifted Grownups: The Mixed Blessings of Extraordinary Potential" (a ten year study of 100 gifted adults). Streznewski [strez NEFF skee] is also a Program Specialist in Gifted Education, and a poet and fiction writer. In our interview, she talked about taking the time she needed to write. Her perspectives can also apply to other creative expression.

"I have four children, a husband and an elderly mother, and now grandchildren, and all of that is a pull of things you care about and want to do," she said. "You have to constantly pull back and say, My writing is important and I must do something for myself, and the world will have to fend for itself for a couple of hours."

She also noted, "The muse may come at a time when it is most inconvenient. One of the ways I have solved that problem over the years is when I'm working on a project, especially a short story, or the novels I've done, I just drag a notebook around with me everywhere."

Hostile environments: corporatism & fundamentalism

Can various kinds of corporate and political actions lead to a "hostile environment" for the free exchange of creative ideas? A hostile environment in a sexual harassment case may include "anything that creates fear, intimidates, ostracizes, psychologically or physically threatens, embarrasses, ridicules…"

A number of thinkers are saying that social forces like corporatism and fundamentalism are exerting increasingly suppressive effects on creative people.

For example, Davidson Loehr [Ph.D.s in philosophy and religion; senior minister of the First Unitarian Universalist Church of Austin] says in his book America, Fascism, and God: "The America that most of us loved has been cleverly and systematically murdered to feed the monetary and imperialistic hunger of some of our greediest people."

Strong stuff. But he notes, "The results of this death are easy to measure. The United States is 49th in the world in literacy and 28th out of 40 countries in mathematical literacy. Europe surpassed the United States in the mid-1990s as the largest producer of scientific literature."

Loehr quotes political scientist Dr. Lawrence Britt, who identifies a list of social and political agendas common to fascist regimes, including: "Religion and government are intertwined; Corporate power is protected; Disdain for intellectuals and the arts."

Of course, just the mere fact of working in a corporate environment does not necessarily mean you are more creatively stifled than someone who is, for example, a freelance writer. And there are some corporations that are notable for encouraging creativity, such as Google.

In her article Creativity and the Meaning of Work, creativity and innovation consultant Linda Naiman writes about corporate attitudes and environments that can stimulate innovation, which is often brought about by multitalented people who are able to make use of their different abilities when encouraged by their workplace.

She notes, "Microsoft is an example of creativity in action. Like many companies born in the Information Age, it is constantly reinventing itself, dissolving old ideas and creating new models and new forms. One of the problems with creativity is that it tends to be chaotic and messy. It grows in a non-linear fashion, like an unruly visitor in the controlled environment of the boardroom. We need to learn to shift our thinking, to work with chaos, because we can no longer avoid it."

In a post on her site, Naiman presents an optimistic view: "The worlds of the arts and business are formulating a new relationship, distinct from the traditional models of entertainment or sponsorship... In this new relationship, art is a role model for business, since all great art pushes boundaries beyond the established norms. Thus, it can teach us about aesthetics, ambiguity, diversity, chaos, change, courage, and complexity."

From her post The art of management | The Economist.

Self-censorship

There are also pressures toward stifling creative expression on a more personal level. For example, being concerned with pleasing others can have a subtle, or even an extensive, impact - acting as an insidious form of self-censorship.

That may be especially an issue for highly sensitive people who react strongly to others' feelings and attitudes.

Ø Ø Ø

RELATIONSHIPS

Solitude or working alone is certainly not the only way to nourish creative projects. Many artists acknowledge the value of academies such as Juilliard, and less formal artist retreats and workshops, like Idyllwild.

Much writing and advice on creative expression and enhancing creativity - including this book - focuses on the inner journey of the individual. But creating happens in a social context, and often depends on inspiration and support from others, on finding an audience, and getting financing from publishers and producers. Creative work impacts other people, even worldwide. But being creative can also be inhibited by others.

Dancer, choreographer and teacher Carol M. Press, Ed.D. writes in her book The Dancing Self that "Creativity's profound effect affirms what binds us together as a species. Creativity contributes immeasurably to the health of humankind; before we understand and accept our differences, we must acknowledge and feel our common bonds...we are social animals, born to live in relation with others."

She adds, "Anthropologist Ellen Dissanayake in her book <u>Art and Intimacy: How the Arts Began</u> asserts that art-making is an intrinsic human capacity that has psychobiological foundations. Through such creative endeavors people experience, express, and elaborate their common interests in finding meaning and competence in their lives."

Dr. Press quotes Dissanayake: "Aesthetic experiences transcend simple short-term self-interest, making us aware of our embeddedness or participation in an expanded frame of reference that is larger than ourselves."

Linda Seger has written a number of books on screenwriting and filmmaking, and talks about the value of "web thinking" in her book with that title. She writes of the emotional and career values of collaboration instead of hierarchy, and networking as a support for one's actualization, not simply a way to make business contacts.

Sally Field has commented that she feels "Actresses and other women in the industry need to have contact with each other. Not to tell sob stories, but to kick each other in the butt creatively." [From my article The Company of Women.]

Other values of social connection include emotional support. Creative expression and personal growth often demand courage and help in dealing with fear.

Referring to a variety of research studies, Robert J. Maurer, PhD, a family therapist, writing consultant and instructor at UCLA, has commented in his classes and books that those people who are able to reach high levels of personal and professional success have a healthy acknowledgment of fear, and they also honor the need to be comforted and supported when extending outside comfort boundaries. [See list of his articles on my site.]

Recognizing and honoring our organic needs for interconnection can help us stay energized and creatively engaged.

But some interactions can inhibit our creativity and talent expression.

Creative people have often been viewed by other kids (and themselves) as outsiders in school, may have suffered from bullying or other hurtful responses from other children, and may still feel that is part of their self concept as adults.

Along with so many other benefits, the **Internet** has allowed us to make connections with people and information to gain more creative inspiration and nourishment, from people anywhere in the world.

Salons and Blogging – developing creativity online

Creative relationships, including romances, have inspired many artists, such as Jean-Paul Sartre and Simone de Beauvoir, Henry Miller and Anais Nin, and Georgia O'Keeffe and Alfred Stieglitz. [These are explored in a book by Vera John-Steiner, Creative Collaboration]

Even casual meetings – parties, wine tastings, dinners, whatever – can also stimulate our creative ideas. Sometimes those meetings become more formalized, such as the Bloomsbury Group in the early 1900s, which included Virginia Woolf, Vita Sackville-West, E. M. Forster, Dora Carrington, Roger Fry and other writers and artists.

In her visually luscious and intellectually stimulating site The Soul Food Cafe, Heather Blakey has a section called Salon du Muse and notes, "Salons are informal gatherings where people talk big talk, talk meant to be listened to and perhaps passionately acted upon. Salons are incubators where ideas are conceived, gestated, and hatched… Salons are the frontiers of social and cultural change… They've been flourishing since ancient Greece."

In her article <u>Zen and the Art of Team Blogging</u> (on another great artist inspiration site, Creativity-Portal.com), she talks about a kind of virtual version of a salon, in which participants "are provided with threads, which inspire them to write or complete artwork… They are given ideas, which are sown and planted and worked with."

Blogs can provide a kind of Salon experience

While the old-style literary salon such as the Bloomsbury Group may be impractical for most of us, blogging can be a way to express ourselves, connect and gain support and inspiration. In my article <u>Gifted Women: Identity and Expression</u>, I note that one of the issues related to being exceptional and creative may be social isolation.

True peer relationships can be rare and demanding. And for those of us who are highly sensitive and disposed to solitary work, isolation can be both protective and a welcome choice. So rather than having to sit around in a "smoky drawing room" to benefit from the creative stimulation of a salon, we have blogs – on our own or in a team – which can be a way to say what we want or need to express, and maybe get creatively stimulating responses.

Do we need solitude or connection for developing creativity?

Some forms of creative expression – like acting and filmmaking – require collaborating with many other people; sometimes an artist needs isolation or works best alone. Writer Erica Jong has commented, "Everyone has a talent. What is rare is the courage to nurture it in solitude and to follow the talent to the dark places where it leads."

Is creating always collaborative?

Keith Sawyer, a professor of psychology and education, says the studies detailed in his book Group Genius: The Creative Power of Collaboration reveal that "creativity is always collaborative – even when you're alone."

According to a Publishers Weekly review, the book shows "how innovation always emerges from a series of sparks—never a single flash of insight…Sawyer looks at how J.R.R. Tolkien and C.S. Lewis composed their epic novels in concert, how unorganized individuals can come together to provide disaster relief more efficiently than government planners, how Charles Darwin and Samuel Morse built their work on others' discoveries, how information sharing helped Silicon Valley beat out Boston's computer startups."

But many people - myself included - are introverted, or for other reasons work best on their own.

"I like to be alone so I can write. But focus can hurt you. I don't want to be some stress casualty in early middle age."
– James Ellroy (crime fiction novelist, "L.A. Confidential" and others).

Both introverted and extroverted

In his post <u>After the Show: The Many Faces of the Performer</u>, creativity researcher Scott Barry Kaufman relates that psychologist Jennifer O. Grimes interviewed musicians at several major summer metal rock tours, including "Ozzfest."

He says that Grimes found that all of the musicians showed interest in physical activities but also reported requiring "alone time." Kaufman also notes, "The introverts in her sample seemed adept at using introversion and extroversion in various facades to manipulate their appearances to the various circles of friends, acquaintances and others. As Grimes puts it, musicians were adept at 'juggling multiple faces' (I really like this way of phrasing it!)."

Cognitive Psychologist Scott Barry Kaufman, PhD is a co-author (with James C. Kaufman, PhD) of The Psychology of Creative Writing.

Is there a need for relationships to be creative?

Psychologist Anne Paris, PhD, author of the book Standing at Water's Edge: Moving Past Fears, Blocks, and Pitfalls to Discover the Power of Creative Immersion, notes "There are most certainly genetic and personality differences in how much connection we need to feel comfortable and at our best. Isolated or introverted artists often have a vivid and alive fantasy life of connecting with others that plays a powerful role in their creative productivity."

She also notes, "Also, these artists may be turning to other types of connections (spirituality, play, pets, and other's artwork) to sustain their work. For some artists at certain times, creative immersion may feel like the safest and most comfortable way of connecting with others, so their creativity flourishes even when they are isolated."

[From interview on her site www.anneparis.com]

Dr. Paris explains in her article A New Approach to Igniting and Sustaining Creativity, "Contrary to how we've been taught to value independence and autonomy, this new scientific evidence is showing that we are at our best when we are connected with others. Applying these findings to the secret, internal world of the artist, the capacity to be creative is actually generated by the experience of connectedness with others."

She details some of the potential reasons that may work for people: "When we are feeling frightened or are lacking self-confidence and vitality, we need to look at the state of our relationships, rather than to blame ourselves for being weak and inadequate, or to think that we must somehow find strength and courage from deep within ourselves. We cannot create in a vacuum of isolation: we are helped along in the creative process by certain kinds of emotional support from others that help us to be at our best and to realize our full potentials."

How others can support your creative work

In her article <u>The Need for Others</u>, Dr. Paris quotes Loren Long, an "accomplished artist who has illustrated many books, including Mr. Peabody's Apples by Madonna, I Dream of Trains by Angela Johnson" and others. "My wife is not an artist, but she has great taste. I run everything by her, sometimes daily as I'm working on a project," Long said.

"She is my first level of screening. If she likes it, then I feel the confidence to proceed. My publishers' opinions are also very important to me. Not just because they determine if my work is adequate. I admire and respect them a lot. I want them to like what I've done. I guess that, in general, I always need someone to like my work. If they don't, my self-doubts come to the surface. You know, like I'm not living up to the grand fantasies I have about myself or about what my work should look like."

Paris notes, "We all need relationships with others to be at our best. When we are surrounded with support, we are more productive, happy, and energetic. Positive relationships also help the artist along in his creative process. Good relationships can bolster our courage to take the plunge into creativity. And likewise, not-so-good relationships, or a lack of relationships, can inhibit our drive."

Have you experienced being helped - or hindered - from your relationships? You may need to regularly demand time and space away from relationships to pursue your creative work.

Ø Ø Ø

> *Limiting*

ADDICTION

This section is not just about drug use and abuse - there are many forms of self-limiting addictive behavior that can interfere with realizing our creative and other talents.

But high ability and substance use is one area to start with. A number of people with exceptional abilities have used drugs, alcohol and other substances - perhaps as self-medication to ease the pain of their sensitivity, or as a way to enhance thinking and creativity. Sometimes they risk addiction. More often, they limit their health and mental clarity needed for creative excellence.

I know something about that from personal experience: a cocaine addiction, successfully treated with cognitive therapy, more than 25 years ago.

Many creative people have had addiction or abuse problems

Beethoven reportedly drank wine about as often as he wrote music, and was an alcoholic or at least a problem-drinker.

Among the many other artists who have used drugs, alcohol or other substances are Aldous Huxley, Samuel Taylor Coleridge, Edgar Allen Poe, Fyodor Dostoevsky, Allen Ginsberg, composer Modest Musorgski, F. Scott Fitzgerald, Raymond Chandler, Eugene O'Neill, Edna St. Vincent Millay, Dorothy Parker, William Faulkner, Ernest Hemingway, Thomas Wolfe, John Steinbeck, and Tennessee Williams. At least five U.S. writers who won the Nobel Prize for Literature have been considered alcoholics.

From my article: Gifted, Talented, Addicted.

Addiction as avoidance

In his richly stimulating article on the philosophy of addiction Unhooked Thinking, William Pryor notes, "I was once a heroin addict. I am now a writer, film producer and entrepreneur, fascinated by the very nature of addiction."

He continues, "Addiction is the map, not the territory. When I was a junky, I learnt to present addiction, to be labelled an addict, because what lay beneath was too difficult, too unacceptable, to express or deal with. So medicalised has become our inner life, so distanced and handed over to figures of authority, that we find it hard to go beyond the map to find the territory within ourselves."

He thinks the "endemic something in the human condition that leads so many to become addicts.. has been called weltschmertz, world-weariness, melancholy and in India, bireh or longing. It is the pain of being human, no more, no less, the pain of having the chaotic self-awareness of human consciousness chained by its attachments to the mundane."

William Pryor is Director of Unhooked Thinking, and author of the book Survival of the Coolest: A Darwin's Death Defying Journey into the Interior of Addiction.

Gifted adults sabotaging with drugs & drink

Actor Robert Downey Jr. has reportedly been clean and sober for a long time, but admits about his long history of drug abuse,

"For years I took pride in being resilient," he says. "But that turned into this guy who can get hit by a brickbat every morning and still look kind of cute. I mean, there's 'ready to be ready,' and then there's waking up in the morning feeling like you've been hit in the back with a sledgehammer."

He is "very very very high maintenance," he admits. "Even without being the inventor of any of my own impediments from this day forward, it's still tough, it's still chaotic."

Another talented actor, Michelle Rodriguez (of the TV series "Lost," the movie "Avatar" and others) was released from a Hawaii jail after being found guilty of drunken driving. She said she was thankful for her arrest "because of the fact that I didn't acknowledge my own behavior and how sporadic it was until all hell broke loose in my life."

That is one of the most insidious aspects of drug and alcohol abuse – losing our capacity to be objective about the destructive results, both on others and ourselves, until it reaches extreme levels. Turner Classic Movies ran a biography on Bette Davis, arguably one of the most gifted and expressive actors, but with a private life that was chaotic, including a marriage to an alcoholic, and being emotionally abusive toward her daughter.

Davis reportedly suffered ill health due to alcohol and cigarette abuse. In many of her films she smoked, as well as in real life; she often lit up on talk shows, and discounted it saying, "If I did not smoke a cigarette, people would not know who I was."

Are gifted and creative people more vulnerable?

In his article: Myth of an 'Addict Gene' (on the huge resource site AddictionInfo.org), Jeffrey Helm writes about some of the issues involved in testing for a supposed genetic vulnerability to addiction.

Helm notes, "Dr. Tom Koch, a bioethicist and professor, is concerned that if a genetic test for addiction were developed, children with genetic risk factors for addiction would be weeded out because only fetuses or embryos free of "deviant" genes would be brought to term. Dr. Koch proposed that screening out unwanted genes is essentially the same as deciding that the world is better off without those genes."

Helm asks, "So is the world better off without people with a biological susceptibility towards becoming addicted? If the answer is yes, Dr. Koch points out that people like Dylan Thomas, William S Burroughs, and Miles Davis might not have existed and brought their art and music into the world. All were artists who struggled with substance abuse."

Can drugs and alcohol enhance creative potential?

When he heard that he was chosen to be the new Bond, actor Daniel Craig says,"I was shopping, and I dropped what I was carrying. I went straight to the alcohol section and got myself a bottle of vodka and a bottle of vermouth and went back and made myself a Martini – or two." [The Sunday Herald, Oct. 16, 2005]

Acclaimed for his toned look as the new James Bond, Craig has commented about his training regime: "I'm not obsessive about fitness. I work out three or four times a week but I take the weekends off and drink as much Guinness as I can get down my neck." [mi6.co.uk]

But that love of knocking down a few – or more – pints he blames for his nude scene in the 2000 movie Some Voices: "The scene was written as me running down the road stripped to the waist covered in tomato juice. But then I got drunk at Simon's and said, 'I'll do it naked!' The lesson is never get drunk with directors." [imdb.com]

Many people enjoy drinking to varying degrees, at times. There are even some health benefits of red wine, for example, that are increasingly supported by research.

But as I note in my article Gifted, Talented, Addicted, the idea of using drugs and alcohol as a way to enhance thinking and creativity can be misguided.

For example, Jane Piirto, Ph.D., Director of Talent Development Education at Ashland University, notes in her article "The Creative Process in Poets" that the "altered mental state brought about by substances has been thought to enhance creativity - to a certain extent." But, she adds, "The danger of turning from creative messenger to addicted body is great, and many writers have succumbed, especially to the siren song of alcohol."

She quotes poet Charles Baudelaire on using alcohol to enhance imagination: "Always be drunk. That is all: it is the question. You want to stop Time crushing your shoulders, bending you double, so get drunk - militantly. How? Use wine, poetry, or virtue, use your imagination. Just get drunk."

One of a number of books by Jane Piirto: Understanding Creativity.

An unconscious strategy that doesn't work in the long-term

Addiction psychologist Marc F. Kern, Ph.D., notes that altering one's state of consciousness is normal and that a destructive habit or addiction is "mostly an unconscious strategy - which you started to develop at a naive, much earlier stage of life - to enjoy the feelings it brought on or to help cope with uncomfortable emotions or feelings. It is simply an adaptation that has gone awry."

My article Gifted, Talented, Addicted also lists a number of articles, books and programs for more information and help.

Ø Ø Ø

CENSORSHIP

One of the most potent forms of censorship of creative work is our own limiting beliefs and negative attitudes. There have been many times in my life when I have stopped pursuing a creative idea, or not even attempted an endeavor, because of my ideas about my capabilities, or the validity of the idea, or many other evaluations. Of course, some of those judgments are realistic and valid - we can't pursue all of our creative concepts.

"The danger of censorship in the United States is less from business or the religious right or the self-righteous left than from the self-censorship of artists themselves, who simply give up." That is a comment by writer and director Frank Pierson (former President of the Academy of Motion Picture Arts and Sciences), who added that there are also external pressures in the marketplace: "If we can't see a way to get out story told, what is the point of trying? I wonder how many fine, inspiring ideas are strangled in the womb of the imagination because there's no way past the gates of commerce." [LA Times May 26, 2003 - quoted in Utne, Sep/Oct 2003.]

But ideas about those "gates of commerce" may be framed in rigid, black-and-white ways, such as "Publishers don't want any more memoirs" (or children's books or whatever) - which become a form of self-limiting thinking.

The point is not that those market forces are not real, but there are usually multiple aspects of a situation. For example, even if all the traditional publishers you've tried have rejected your book proposal, why not self-publish?

Censoring – both internal and external – is discussed by Eric Maisel, PhD in his article

<u>Are You Censoring Yourself?</u> – in which he talks about an artist's relationship to society.

"Most of us would be quick to say that we are free to think just about anything and to express ourselves in any way we see fit," he writes.

"In reality, artists do a lot of measuring, somewhere just out of conscious awareness, about what is safe or seemly to reveal and what is unsafe or unseemly. One aspect of this self-censorship is the way we bite our tongue at our day job and, in a corollary safety measure, skip making art that reveals what our corporation, institution, or agency is up to."

In his book <u>Mastering Creative Anxiety</u>, he further explains how making choices about which creative work to pursue - and therefore what to leave aside or postpone - can be an ongoing source of stress and anxiety. He also details specific strategies to deal with anxiety.

Natalie Rogers on politics & creative expression

Author, artist and psychotherapist Natalie Rogers, Ph.D. says the focus in her professional work has been to "give an active life" to her father Carl Rogers' "Theory of Creativity." She has commented about censorship, "In these times where conformity is being thrust upon us by governments, we urgently need strong individuals who are able to think and act creatively."

She adds, "Creativity threatens those who demand conformity. Dictators squelch self-expression and the creative process. They do not want their citizens to think for themselves or to be spontaneous, imaginative or self-determined. Thus, creativity is subversive to those who demand conformity to a political system."

From article: Giving Life to Carl Rogers Theory of Creativity – by Natalie Rogers, Ph.D. Her book, The Creative Connection: Expressive Art as Healing, "joins person-centered theory and the expressive arts to facilitate deep inner work."

But it isn't just dictators; some corporations and other institutions are also political systems which may pressure people toward conformity and away from creativity and innovation.

Artists and censorship – fighting for creative expression

In addition to endless ways we can self-limit and self-censor our creative expression, there are often subtle – and not so subtle – forms of censorship that can impact creative endeavors, sometimes even before they can find an audience.

One example was the refusal of TV network NBC to run ads for the Dixie Chicks documentary "Shut Up & Sing" a number of years ago, which included footage of lead singer Natalie Maines saying during a concert in 2003 that the band was "ashamed" to come from the same state, Texas, as President George Bush. Many country music radio stations also refused to play the Dixie Chicks' records, and some even boycotted ads for their "Accidents & Accusations" tour, "leading the band to cancel numerous dates in the South and Midwest." [Reuters/VNU Fri Oct 27 2006.]

In her AlterNet post "The Sexist Backlash Against the Dixie Chicks," Melissa Silverstein [Women's Media Center] comments about their new album: "Recording it and writing their own songs for the first time functioned as a catharsis for the hell they went through. Their dismay with the country world is clear in the first single, 'Not Ready to Make Nice,' an anthem of unrepentant anger. Theirs is the best sort of feminist story: all about what happens when women stand up for what they believe in. At the end of the documentary, [Director Barbara] Kopple shows the Dixie Chicks returning to the arena in London where the controversy began. Maines restates her comment, this time with a big smile on her face."

The post adds that Kopple got to know her subjects well while following them around for over a year. "I think, more than anything," Kopple says, "their experience has highlighted that — although the cost of speaking your mind and being yourself can be high — the cost of being silenced is much higher."

Many musicians and other artists have been censored

An Excerpt from a summary of the book Taboo Tunes: A History of Banned Bands & Censored Songs notes there have been "firestorms of controversy that have engulfed brave artists like Woody Guthrie, Paul Robeson, Billie Holiday, Elvis Presley, the Beatles, the Rolling Stones, Jimi Hendrix, the Dead Kennedy's, Madonna, N.W.A., Public Enemy, Ice-T, Nirvana, the Dixie Chicks.. and many others."

George Orwell wrote in the preface to his book "Animal Farm" that the "chief danger to freedom of thought and speech...is not the direct interference of the MOI [the British Ministry of Information] or any official body. If publishers and editors exert themselves to keep certain topics out of print, it is not because they are frightened of prosecution but because they are frightened of public opinion. In this country, intellectual cowardice is the worst enemy a writer or journalist has to face."

And Ray Bradbury, author of "Fahrenheit 451" once commented, "You don't have to burn books to destroy a culture; just get people to stop reading them."

Ø Ø Ø

PERFECTIONISM - CRITICISM

Striving for excellence can refine our work, but being perfectionistic to an extreme degree or in unhealthy ways can seriously impact our creativity and creative expression. So can taking on other people's criticism as valid even when it isn't. At times, I have noticed, some of my own perfectionism is based on other people's values and standards more than mine. Becoming aware of that has been helpful to me in my writing, for example. Of course, there are standards of writing style that generally need to be followed in order to assure one's ideas are expressed clearly and accurately. But "coloring outside the lines" also has its place.

Perfect is bogus

As performance psychology consultant John Eliot, PhD notes in his article <u>Reverse Psychology for Success</u> "There is no ideal; there is no perfect. Striving for either is a sure fire way to tie yourself up in knots. I tell performers all the time: Perfectionism is simply putting a limit on your future. When you have an idea of perfect in your mind, you open the door to constantly comparing what you have now with what you want, how you are performing now with how you want to perform. That type of self criticism is significantly deterring."

He explains, "The idea of perfect closes your mind to new standards. When you drive hard toward one ideal, you miss opportunities and paths, not to mention hurting your confidence. Believe in your potential and then go out and explore it; don't limit it."

He notes that Richard Branson, Bill Gates, Michael Dell "first believed in themselves, utterly, and let their belief be their guide. Sure they experienced numerous obstacles and setbacks and failures. Confidence allowed them to keep getting up and looking for ways to move forward."

John Eliot, Ph.D. is author of the book Overachievement: The New Model for Exceptional Performance.

Letting go of perfectionism

Ellie Drake is CEO of BraveHeart Productions; a keynote speaker, coach, doctor, and successful entrepreneur. In her article Are You Aware?, she writes, "For me, being a perfectionist brings about an instant self criticism component. I am glad to say that I have learned to be good to myself. Therefore, I have realized that to let go of perfectionism, means to get out of the way, and perform to the best of my ability in the moment."

It may be possible to use perfectionism in the pursuit of excellence, but she notes that we may be holding ourselves back by waiting "till we are good" and that "We must first do, and then we will be good." She also finds that "perfectionism is one of the biggest blocks to creativity. I have also learned when I am creative, I accomplish more. When I accomplish more, I feel good. But to be creative, I now know that I must first feel good. Perfectionism is the stop sign. It is the resistance in the way."

Inside Out or Outside In

Lisa Erickson, MS, LMHC, a psychotherapist with interests including the relationship between giftedness, addiction and trauma, notes there are different sources and dynamics of perfectionism.

She writes, "The gifted person is driven to express their interests and pursuits. Perfectionism is about passion, energy, and focus…If their creative endeavor falls short, the gifted person pushes onward to get as close as they can to what they envision. Perfectionism is connected to developmental potential and entelechy. It is the determination to be the best one can be."

This type of perfectionism, she says, is "rooted internally in giftedness." It is intrinsic and moves from the "inside out."

But, she adds, "Another type of perfectionism is rooted in having an impaired parent (or two). This type of perfectionism is a response to outside circumstances. It is a consequence of abandonment and neglect. Its source is external."

She explains more about the differences and how to work with perfectionism, or heal unhealthy forms, in her article Perfectionism: From the inside out or the outside in?

Also see more perfectionism articles

Undercutting ourselves in other ways

"Don't compromise yourself. You're all you've got." - Janis Joplin

But don't we do that? Compromise, stifle ourselves, shut down what we are capable of? I know I do at times.

Having multiple talents inherently means making choices to pursue and realize some abilities, and not others - perhaps many others. And that kind of choosing may arouse fears, disappointment and other feelings about paths not taken, possibilities not fulfilled.

"You may feel like dwelling on your limits or your fears. Don't do it... A perfect prescription for a squandered, unfulfilled life is to accommodate self-defeating feelings while undercutting your finest, most productive ones." ~ Marsha Sinetar, in her book "To Build the Life You Want, Create the Work You Love."

That sort of self-limiting attention on what is deficient or unrealized about our abilities is all too easy for many high ability people to do. Especially if you have a tendency toward perfectionism.

Toxic Criticism and developing creativity

In one of his podcast series, Eric Maisel notes "Criticism is a real crippler. I'm sure that you know that. But you may not be aware just how powerful a negative force criticism can be, how much damage it can do to your self-confidence, or how seriously it can deflect you from your path. Almost nothing does more psychological damage than criticism."

He explains that criticism and self-criticism "come at us from the past, as bad memories and as our own introjected 'inner critic.' It comes at us every day, at work and at home. It even colors our sense of the future. Some of it is minor and only ruffles our feathers a little bit. But a surprising amount of it is toxic, as bad for our system as any poison." Continued in his article Introducing Toxic Criticism.

Healthy criticism or self-criticism can help refine our creative talents, but when it is based on excessive perfectionism or an unrealistic self concept, criticism of ourselves can be destructive and self-limiting, eroding our creative assurance and vitality.

Highly creative and talented people are often susceptible to perfectionism and unreasonably high standards and expectations that can lead to this exaggerated criticism. See more in my article Being Creative and Self-critical.

Ø Ø Ø

PRESSURE TO PERFORM

The pressures to fulfill talents and creative potential

For those with exceptional abilities, there are often multiple pressures – from family, the culture, oneself – to continuously "produce" or achieve at a high level.

Alissa Quart is the author of <u>Hothouse Kids: The Dilemma of the Gifted Child</u>. A newspaper article noted Quart is "the only child of two academics who prized education and intelligence. She read at age 3 and wrote her first novel when she was 7, and writes about pressures put on children, especially gifted children and prodigies, that encourage perfectionism, performance anxiety and lifelong feelings of not being able to keep up."

Her father especially, Quart said, was "hell-bent on bettering my lot — and by extension our family's lot — and keep me from languishing in what he considered the Blank Generation."

The article says that to achieve this aim, he drilled her on such cultural trivia as the names of B-movie actresses, and on revolutionary movements and vocabulary.

"Some parents see gifted children as some sort of insurance as they try to navigate the middle class without a safety net," Quart said. "With so much competition for everything from the best summer camps to permanent jobs, children are working harder than ever to achieve and so are their parents, as they use their gifted child to attain class mobility or to ensure the family's place in the social strata, she writes.

The article adds, "Quart names this pressure to achieve the 'Icarus Effect,' after the story of Icarus. who flew too high, the wings melted and he fell to the sea. While Quart never fell into the sea, she said she struggled with a 'distinct feeling of failure' as she grew older, in part because of the high expectations placed on her."

[From "Prodigies and the push to excel," by Debora Vrana, Los Angeles Times Sept 30 2006.]

I have not read Hothouse Kids, but it seems from the above article that the author is raising important issues that can and do affect highly talented people throughout their lives –

issues such as perfectionism, self-limiting, anxiety, self concept and mental health.

How the Pygmalion Effect transforms our creative potential

In George Bernard Shaw's play "Pygmalion" (and the musical "My Fair Lady"), Professor Henry Higgins claims he can transform Cockney flower girl Eliza Doolittle into a duchess. Eliza realizes "the difference between a lady and a flower girl is not how she behaves but how she's treated." [From article The Pygmalion Effect by Eric Garner.]

Dr. Robert Rosenthal [formerly of Harvard University] conducted formal studies on self-fulfilling prophecies, and what became known as the Pygmalion Effect: How teachers' expectations affect student performance. In an experimental situation, some teachers are told they are the best in their school, and "as a special reward" will be teaching a group of the brightest students.

As summarized in the article Positive Expectancy, "At the end of the school year, these students led not only the school, but the entire school district in academic accomplishment."

But actually, both teachers and their students had been selected at random, not chosen for high ability. Their achievement was an outcome of positive expectation for success. This powerful influence of a self-fulfilling prophecy may not only impact how others flourish, but ourselves.

Personal development leader Brian Tracy includes the Pygmalion Effect research in his program The Psychology of Achievement.

Maybe a variation on this is the "law of attraction" and the power of belief as presented in "The Secret." In his article Notes on The Secret DVD, Bob Proctor declares that "all the great leaders all down through history, as far back as you want to go, have complete and unanimous agreement on one point, that we become what we think about. We have the freedom to think anything we want, we can originate thoughts or we can pick thoughts just out of the ether, and we can internalize those thoughts; we can bring them together and build beautiful ideas, or we can build terrible ideas."

Born with talent - or not?

Carol S. Dweck, PhD, a Professor of Psychology at Stanford University, writes in an issue of the Duke Gifted Letter:

* Some people are born gifted, and others are not.

* You can tell who will be gifted from early on.

* Gifted children should be labeled and praised for their brains and talent.

She says, "All of these statements are accepted by many as true. However, as evidence has accumulated over the past decade, another view has been gaining credence that portrays giftedness as a more dynamic quality that can grow or stagnate."

In her book Mindset: The New Psychology of Success, she details the growth mindset: "The hand you're dealt is just the starting point for development. This growth mindset is based on the belief that your basic qualities are things you can cultivate through your efforts."

See more in my posts Carol Dweck on developing creative talent and Carol Dweck on the growth mindset.

Expectation about ability, success and other key issues, is also a matter of our overall attitude and emotional stance toward life.

In her article Are You Settling?, Valerie Young quotes noted playwright, poet and former Czech president Vaclac Havel: "Hope is an orientation of the spirit, an orientation of the heart. It is not the conviction that something will turn out well, but the certainty that something makes sense, regardless of how it turns out."

A profile of Young notes, "Since escaping her corporate job in 1995 to found Changing Course, 'Dreamer in Residence Dr. Valerie Young's career advice has appeared around the world." She provides many workshops and other resources for entrepreneurs and others who want to realize their talents. Her site theme is "Discovering Interesting Ways to Make a Living Doing What You Love Is Easier Than You Think."

Ø Ø Ø

SCHOOLING

School and formal education can incubate our passions to achieve. But it can also instill self-limiting patterns of thinking and behavior.

Robert Kiyosaki recalls his early school years: "Today I don't use much of what I learned after the fifth grade. But that's not to say school didn't leave its permanent mark on me. The fact is, I left school with several behavioral traits I hadn't walked in with."

Writing in the book Einstein's Business: Engaging Soul, Imagination and Excellence in the Workplace, he continues: "Engraved in my mind was the belief that making a mistake, or 'screwing up,' got me ridiculed by my peers and often my teacher. School brainwashed me into believing that if a person wanted to be successful in life, he or she had to always be right. In other words, never be wrong."

He adds, "School taught me to avoid being wrong (making mistakes) at all costs. And if you did happen to make a mistake, at least be smart enough to cover it up. This is where all too many people are today—not allowing themselves to make mistakes and thus blocking their own progress."

This urge toward unhealthy perfectionism can deeply affect us, he notes: "The symptoms of this 'disease' are feelings of boredom, failure, and dissatisfaction, although most of us never come to understand why we feel this way. After having it drilled into us for so many years, it's hard to imagine that being 'right' could cause such unhappiness."

Robert Kiyosaki is an investor, businessman, motivational speaker, and self-help author of Rich Dad, Poor Dad, and Rich Dad Secrets.

But perfectionism is not entirely "evil" - it can help fuel our pursuit of excellence. See the preceding chapter Perfectionism - Criticism and the articles In Praise of Perfectionism by

Stephen A. Diamond, Ph.D., and my article Perfectionism.

Patterns of thinking and behavior that hold us back

In his book Your Own Worst Enemy: Breaking the Habit of Adult Underachievement, psychologist Kenneth W. Christian, PhD talks about styles or patterns of thinking and behavior that we probably developed in school, and that solidify into ruts that can limit our fulfillment, achievement and creativity.

One example is a group of people he calls Extreme Non-Risk-Takers – who "focus totally on minimizing risk in their lives… because they try to avoid situations in which they could possibly fail, they gravitate toward occupations, relationships and activities that do not present serious challenges or reflect their real interests."

I experienced some of that pattern when I failed Organic Chemistry in college, and - in addition to the blow to my self-esteem - considered it a "message" that I was not meant to be a physician. Addled adolescent thinking, more than clear judgment.

Another pattern and group, also related to perfectionism for some people, is Self-Doubters / Self-Attackers – who "block their success by holding high standards they feel they can never possibly meet and for which they therefore seldom strive."

More styles include: Charmers; Rebels ; Misunderstood Geniuses; Best-or-Nothings. Read more about them on the page Self-limiting. Also see articles by Kenneth Christian.

Educated out of our creativity

Our self concept, recognition of our talents, appreciation for divergent thinking and pursuit of creativity can be guided and nurtured, or corroded and even corrupted, by our school experiences.

In his article Do schools kill creativity?, Sir Ken Robinson notes that "kids will take a chance. If they don't know, they'll have a go. They're not frightened of being wrong. Now, I don't mean to say that being wrong is the same thing as being creative. What we do know is, if you're not prepared to be wrong, you'll never come up with anything original."

He notes that by the time "they get to be adults, most kids have lost that capacity. They have become frightened of being wrong… And the result is, we are educating people out of their creative capacities." He notes, "Picasso once said that all children are born artists. The problem is to remain an artist as we grow up. I believe this passionately, that we don't grow into creativity, we grow out of it. Or rather we get educated out of it."

Related post with video: <u>Sir Ken Robinson: Do schools kill creativity?</u>

My related article <u>Getting out of school alive</u>.

Ø Ø Ø

WORK AND CAREER

Aside from school (not just education, which hopefully lasts your whole life), work is an area of your life where you can make use of your multiple talents - or at least some of them.

I am including it here, in the **Limiting** section, though, because for many people, the pressures of making a living, and the political and social climate of business, especially large corporations, can stifle creative expression.

For example, in one of my corporate jobs many years ago, a customer service position for a cellular phone company, I had some ideas I thought might be of interest to the engineering research and development division, so I sent an executive a note. Which resulted in my being chastised by my immediate supervisor for not going through her - even though she had no apparent interest in or understanding of the engineering technology.

A trivial example, perhaps, but how many potentially creative or stimulating ideas have been shunted aside or not even expressed because a particular corporate climate was discouraging?

But here are some other points about how to more fully find and express talents in the area of work and career.

Changing your job can be a stimulus to pursue creative passions

Designer Susan Kirkland, for example, in her Graphic Design Forum blog post Separations, talks about the creative pleasures of freelancing, but also a common challenge: "If you get the axe, or you're canned, fired, sacked, terminated, dismissed, discharged or even euphemistically, laid off; don't despair because your new found freedom may just be the spark you need to change your life."

Author and workshop leader Valerie Young notes in her article Are You Settling? that making positive changes in our lives is not necessarily a straight path: "If you are serious in your intention to change course, you must do so with a hopeful spirit. Expect bumps in the road. At the same time, have faith that even if the reason is not clear at the time, everything really does makes sense. You don't have to wait to turn 50 to experience the serenity and the power that comes with knowing what you want. Life is just too short to settle for less."

One of the Changing Course programs is: Finding Your True Calling.

Career concerns for multitalented people

One of my experiences in life has been questioning (and feeling anxious at times) about why I have not fit in to any mainstream corporate or even entrepreneurial career roles - though over the past few years I have been more and more "serious" and focused about making money by helping others find useful information for personal growth and business development.

Part of this issue is having so many intellectual and creative interests, and not having the focus or motivation to build a well-defined career. This affects many people, I suspect - especially those of you drawn to reading this book.

One framework for this is what Barbara Sher identified as being a "Scanner." It may be an awkward name, but as described on Barbara Sher's Genius Press site, a Scanner is "Someone fascinated by so many areas she can't settle for only one."

A page on the site for the April 2011 Scanner's Retreat in France, explains the term was first described in Sher's New York Times Best Seller "I Could Do Anything If I Only Knew What it Was" and later in her newer book "Refuse to Choose!: A Revolutionary Program for Doing Everything That You Love" - and that 'Scanners' refers to "Renaissance men and women, eclectic experts, happy amateurs and delighted dilettantes."

In my post Are you a scanner personality? Maybe all you need is a good enough job, I quote her on the satisfaction of doing work that fits your personality and values - and on not having everything you do tied to money.

Sher says "A good enough job is a subsidy to the art. There are a number of things you want to do when you're a Scanner, or a talented person, that will never pay money, or if they do, they won't pay money for years. You don't want to hitch the profit wagon to everything you're talented at. Lots of Scanners have a lot of fun with a good enough job. Look at clerks in books stores. When somebody loves books, that's a Scanner."

But that can probably also apply to multi-millionaire entrepreneurs and corporate leaders like Steve Jobs and Martha Stewart and Steven Spielberg - not that I know any of them, but at least in public appearances, they seem to be experiencing a lot of joy and satisfaction in what they do. On the other hand, one or all of those examples may not be Scanners.

Barbara Sher explains in her article What is a Scanner?, that "Scanners love to read and write, to fix and invent things, to design projects and businesses, to cook and sing, and to create the perfect dinner party. (You'll notice I didn't use the word "or," because Scanners don't love to do one thing or the other; they love them all.) A Scanner might be fascinated with learning how to play bridge or bocce, but once she gets good at it, she might never play it again. One Scanner I know proudly showed me a button she was wearing that said, 'I Did That Already.'

"To Scanners the world is like a big candy store full of fascinating opportunities, and all they want is to reach out and stuff their pockets. It sounds wonderful, doesn't it? The problem is, Scanners are starving in the candy store. They believe they're allowed to pursue only one path. But they want them all. If they force themselves to make a choice, they are forever discontented."

One problem with this sort of multitude of high abilities and interests, she notes, is that "usually Scanners don't choose anything at all. And they don't feel good about it."

Not simply "not good" - but possibly suffering with seriously compromised self-esteem and self-concept, not to mention chronic dissatisfaction, along with stress and anxiety. It doesn't help that most of us live in a culture (the U.S.) that so unrelentingly promotes the idea of "finding your place" and discovering "what you are meant to do" - then training for it and sticking with it.

Of course, we are all different, and being a Scanner personality - or multitalented in other ways - does not mean we are automatically out of place or suffering from having so many interests. But from the reading I have done in this area, there is definitely a vulnerability for many of us.

For more, see one of my related posts: Realizing multiple passions.

Ø Ø Ø

HEALING

One of the values in using creative talents is to explore our inner selves and deep emotional needs, rather than ignoring or delaying greater self-understanding in favor of the more mundane stuff of life. "Discovering" the Internet about 15 years ago, especially learning how to publish on the World Wide Web, has been a deeply valuable experience - helping relieve my anxieties and depression, find more meaning in my work, and better define my real interests and passions and identity.

Writer Anne Lamott notes in her acclaimed book "Bird by Bird" that writing in general can be "dealing with the one thing you've been avoiding all along – your wounds." And, she adds, "This is very painful. It stops a lot of people early on who didn't get into this for the pain. They got into it for the money and the fame. So they either quit, or they resort to a type of writing that is sort of like candy making."

But those who go ahead and write and make other creative projects in spite of pain and discomfort, developing creations that explore authentic depths, can enjoy the satisfaction of enriching both themselves and the audience.

Some related books on deep personal writing:
Inner Journeying Through Art-journaling; Writing and Being: Embracing Your Life Through Creative Journaling

Healing ourselves and others through creative expression

Artist Roxanne Chinook has had personal experiences of rape and family violence, and has said her art "emulates a personal and cultural experience, from the spirit of the trickster to healing from the traumas of my past. The process of creating strengthens and restores my spirit, and has rendered me a relationship with the sacred."

As I note in my article The Alchemy of Art, creative expression can transform painful reactions and situations, providing strength and understanding to change how we feel and interact with the world.

And works of art made by others can remodel our inner realities. A newspaper article talks about screenwriter Kimberly Lofstrom Johnson's writing of her drama "Curve" [in development as a movie] about a young woman threatened by a psychopathic hitchhiker. She wrote the story following a year undergoing radiation therapy for Hodgkin's lymphoma.

"It was definitely inspired by my experience being sick," she notes. "Being sick is a lot like being trapped. I wouldn't want to put myself through torture like that again," she says, referring to the therapy. "But then again, the best stuff that you do comes from whatever amount of pain and emotion you've experienced."

From "Scary tale has a scarier subtext" by Jay A. Fernandez, Los Angeles Times January 3, 2007. See more quotes, books, articles on my site page healing & art.

Being creative to save ourselves

In the "Hustle and Flow" post on her Blast O' Joy blog, business coach Suzanne Falter-Barns praises this "incredible indie film about a drug dealing pimp in the backwaters of Memphis who lives his dream of becoming a successful rapper." She says, "I found a lot of inspiration here for dream pursuit – and you will, too. It conveys one of my key messages – that your creative self-expression is the fast road to healing. It can give you back your mojo in about one minute when you connect to that magical spirit – even when you're a down and out pimp having a mid life crisis. You can just feel that passion that pours through his soul." [The film stars Terrence Howard who was also outstanding in "Crash" and other movies.]

Psychiatrist Judith Orloff M.D. comments in her book Positive Energy: "Creativity is the mother of all energies, nurturer of your most alive self. It charges up every part of you. This energy rises from your own life force and from a larger spiritual flow."

Many artists and other people acknowledge that this energy of creative expression helps them deal with life, even heal from physical, emotional, sexual abuse.

"The portal of healing and creativity always takes us into the realm of the spirit" notes Angeles Arrien, author of The Nine Muses: A Mythological Path to Creativity.

But on the other side, suppressing or being blocked from creative expression can be emotionally toxic or destructive, leading to ills such as depression, as psychologist and creativity coach Eric Maisel makes clear in his book The Van Gogh Blues.

Self-Care and creative expression

Creative expression involves our whole being, so taking care of ourselves emotionally, spiritually and physically is part of being a healthy and thriving creative person.

Musician Henry Rollins commented about being a performer and staying healthy while doing road tours with his Rollins Band: "Eating well is becoming easier on the road as more places are health conscious. Gyms are easy to find anywhere there's electricity and traffic."

But, he added, "Time is the hard part. I do my best and I learned a long time ago that without recuperative sleep, good nutrition and constant exercise, this high stress lifestyle of traveling, etc., quickly takes a toll. And how do I do it? I just see it as a very important thing and make sure I get it done."

Continued in my Creative Mind blog post Taking Care of Your Creative Self

Ø Ø Ø

MEANING

This is another of the "big topics" just touched on in this book. Like passion, meaning is another central element in how we choose which of our talents to develop and express.

Or choose not to: If it isn't meaningful in some way to use a talent, why bother? Well, maybe if you get paid a lot for doing it... Not really.

Finding and making meaning is especially crucial for creative people, and one of the potential consequences of insufficient meaning in our lives and work is depression.

Psychologist and creativity coach Eric Maisel, PhD points out in his article Making Meaning that the ongoing search for meaning and the task of meaning-making "is work, but it is the loving work of self-creation. It is the choice we make about how we intend to live our life."

And in his book The Van Gogh Blues: A Creative Person's Path Through Depression, Maisel notes, "Creators have trouble maintaining meaning. Creating is one of the ways they endeavor to maintain meaning. In the act of creation, they lay a veneer of meaning over meaninglessness and sometimes produce work that helps others maintain meaning." He warns that "not creating is depressing because creators are not making meaning when they are not creating."

Author, artist, performer, and creativity coach Janet Riehl interviewed Eric Maisel, PhD about his book in her article: Eric Maisel's "Van Gogh Blues" Explores Connection and

Meaning-making as Treatments for Depression.

[Also see it on her site riehlife.com, with additional links.]

Here is an excerpt:

Janet Riehl: "Eric, what I hear you saying is that when creative people in particular maintain a connection to their mission or purpose (you call it a Life Purpose Statement in "Van Gogh Blues"), a connection to the value of their work, and their own value as creative people in the culture, they will be stronger in their work and in their lives. Is that a fair way to put it?"

Eric Maisel: "Yes. Even before you can make meaning, you must nominate yourself as the meaning-maker in your own life and fashion a central connection with yourself, one that is more aware, active, and purposeful than the connection most people fashion with themselves."

Making the most of our talents

Elsewhere, Maisel writes in a sample from his Meaning Solution Program: "Self-actualization is a lovely word that stands for our desire to make the most of our talents. Instead of using only a small portion of your total being, just enough to get by, you make the conscious decision to employ your full intelligence, your emotional capital, and your best personality qualities in the service of growth and good works. We know that we'd love to make use of our potential and make ourselves proud. Self-actualization is the way you become your real self and your best self. You will do yourself a great service if you treat self-actualization as one of your most important meaning opportunities."

Dr. Maisel has also created the field of existential cognitive-behavioral therapy (ECBT), which he says is "the technical name for a field where meaning, thoughts, and behavior come together." The Meaning Solution Program he developed "spells out what a meaning problem is and does more than identify generic solutions—it walks you step-by-step to your own personal solution."

Read more on my Personal Growth Information site page: The Meaning Solution Program – by Eric Maisel.

Photographer Annie Leibovitz

A newspaper article commented about Leibovitz' preparation for her new book, a mix of her personal and celebrity shots, "A Photographer's Life: 1990-2005," that she had pinned shots on a wall "from her magazine assignments – celebrity portraits that have become icons of American pop culture and have made her one of the world's best-known photographers."

"I was just so overwhelmed by what I was finding in the personal work, because this is who I am," said Leibovitz, who invested a year or more sorting through the pictures. Her famous work for Vanity Fair magazine and other publications "seemed troublingly formal and less intimate," she said, adding: "I could barely look at the assignment wall."

The article adds that Leibovitz is proud of this work, "But, she said ruefully, she wished it 'had more meaning. Had more substance.' Beginning with her photos for Rolling Stone in the 1970s, Leibovitz has produced some of the most memorable images in recent history: a naked John Lennon curled around Yoko Ono, taken hours before he was killed; a naked and very pregnant Demi Moore staring boldly into the camera; Whoopi Goldberg in a tub filled with milk." [From "Essentially Annie" by Josh Getlin, Los Angeles Times, October 11, 2006.]

Laura Berman Fortgang and Mark Fortgang on meaning

An aspiring actress turned interfaith minister, life coach and personal growth author,

Laura Berman Fortgang relates in her book
The Little Book on Meaning: Why We Crave It,
How We Create It a story about the Dalai Lama
addressing a group of scientists and saying
"Curiosity is part of my life, part of my self.
Look at this body. Some areas have more hair,
some less. Why?"

Fortgang continues, "Instead of
answering the question, he stopped at the
question. It is this feeling of wonder, openness,
and curiosity that can give birth to so much as
long as we can get comfortable exploring the
vastness of the unanswered questions."

She adds, "Leading life in a meaningful
way requires embracing the empty spaces, the
blanks and vastness. Living in the gap, we find
ourselves."

Isn't that a poetic phrase: "Living in the
gap"? That refers, I think, to a state of mind
and being that many creative people share.

You can view a video she produced
(with her husband) on my page Meaning and
Purpose.

Ø Ø Ø

VISUALIZATION

Using all our senses to improve performance

Creating images and ideas of what you want to accomplish can be a powerful strategy for achievement, according to many writers, coaches and research studies. Perhaps the most research has been about athletes, but artists can use the technique or approach as well.

Actor Dennis Haysbert has portrayed a variety of dynamic characters in film (such as "Jarhead") and television (including "24" and "The Unit"). "I visualize the roles that I want," he says. "If I hadn't visualized playing athletes, I wouldn't have gotten 'Major League.' If I hadn't visualized playing a president, David Palmer never would have happened. You've got to have a sense of what you want to do; otherwise, the universe is just going to throw something at you." [TV Guide, July 3-9 2006.]

In her article Awakening the Senses, creativity coach Linda Dessau writes about the book "How to think like Leonardo da Vinci" by Michael Gelb, particularly the "Sensazione" chapter, which Dessau notes "is dedicated to re-awakening and sharpening each of the five senses: sight, sound, smell, taste and touch." She adds, "Gelb offers lots of exercises in this chapter to help you awaken your senses. My favourite is 'Subtle Speculation: The Art of Visualization'. As he explains: 'The ability to visualize a desired outcome is built into your brain, and your brain is designed to help you succeed in matching that picture with your performance. And the more thoroughly you involve all your senses, the more compelling your visualization becomes.'"

Other teachers and writers who talk about the power of visualization include Shakti Gawain, author of Creative Visualization, and Wayne Dyer, author of The Power of Intention

Different kinds of visualization

The nature of it can be a key element in how effective visualization is. A PsyBlog article refers to research on imagining the processes involved in reaching a goal, rather than just the end-state of achieving it. UCLA researchers Lien B. Pham and Shelley E. Taylor had students "either visualize their ultimate goal of doing well in an exam or the steps they would take to reach that goal, such as studying.

The results were clear, says the article. "Participants who visualized themselves reading and gaining the required skills and knowledge, spent longer actually studying and got better grades in the exam. (Interestingly, though, the relationship generally found between time spent studying and good grades is surprisingly weak.) There were two reasons that visualizing the process worked: Planning: visualizing the process helped focus attention on the steps needed to reach the goal. Emotion: process visualization led to reduced anxiety." [From article: The Right Kind of Visualisation, PsyBlog.]

That last reason is interesting: How many times do we slow down or set aside our pursuit of a talent out of some kind of anxiety over not being able to do it "well enough" (perfectionism) or having to give up other talents and interests, or some other anxiety-producing belief?

The confabulation of art

Painter Robert Genn notes a definition of confabulation is "the confusion of imagination with memory, and/or the confusion of true memories with false memories." So what does that have to do with visualization?

In his article Marvelous confabulation, painter Robert Genn writes, "Perhaps it's only with the addition of confabulation that art delivers its wizardry and magic. Early researchers, such as psychologist Daniel Berlyne (1972), linked confabulation with amnesia and abnormal brain chemistry. Nowadays it's more pleasantly harnessed to the marvelous potential of the human imagination. Fantastic and spontaneous outpourings of irrelevant associations and bizarre ideas come quite naturally to ordinary creative folks."

Genn thinks "Art without confabulation is the plain goods. Confabulatory enhancement can come from an idiosyncratic style or stroke, or from some happenstance slice from an individualist's hand. It can also come from the brain. Ancillary ideas, metaphors and the embellishments of truth add interest and depth to otherwise standard work."

One point of this is that many kinds of artists make use of their mental abilities to "confabulate" in their creative work - and maybe those abilities can be extended to other talents and areas of personal development.

Ø Ø Ø

INTENTION

Creative expression and the power of intention

Author Wayne Dyer, among many other personal development writers and experts, affirms the power of intention in realizing talents, and says it is "the difference between motivation and inspiration. Motivation is when you get hold of an idea and don't let go of it until you make it a reality. Inspiration is the reverse – when an idea gets hold of you and you feel compelled to let that impulse or energy carry you along. You get to a point where you realize that you're no longer in charge, that there's a driving force inside you that can't be stopped. Look at the great athletes, musician, artists, and writers. They all tap into a source." [Family Circle, June 2005]

The way Dyer is talking about motivation and inspiration sounds to me close to some of the ideas presented earlier in the chapter on Obsession - Perseverance. Like other people, one of the ways I have been energized to keep pursuing a creative idea or project is this "impulse or energy." We may not even be able to get started without that sort of power.

Dyer's related book is <u>The Power of Intention</u>. Dyer also advises in his book <u>10 Secrets for Success and Inner Peace</u>, "Refuse to allow yourself to have low expectations about what you're capable of creating. As Michelangelo suggested, the greater danger is not that your hopes are too high and you fail to reach them; it's that they're too low and you do."

You can find books and programs by Wayne Dyer and many other personal growth authors at <u>Nightingale-Conant</u>.

Choosing intention

In his article <u>The Power of a Clear Intention</u>, writer Kinney Dancair notes that embracing our purpose and choosing to set a clear intention to fulfill it is powerful: "While it can't be proven that every person who has ever set a clear intention got what they were after, it can be shown – empirically mind you – that no real success has been wrought from uncertain intentions."

As an example, he notes "While George Lucas may not have known that film was where his talent lay in the beginning, once he learned the talent was there, he pursued it from then on by choice, not by accident. The list of luminaries who prove this rule is indefinably long."

But psychologist Kenneth W. Christian, Ph.D. cautions, "Regardless of what you choose, your choices have a consequence. Exercise care about your choice. Then think. What am I doing with my time? What do I need to do to express who I am and actualize what I have to give? Pick one new thing to do each day that expresses the intention to raise your standard of living."

Dr. Christian is author of the book Your Own Worst Enemy: Breaking the Habit of Adult Underachievement. See more about his work at his site Maximum Potential Project maxpotential.com. Also see excerpts from his book on my site page Self-limiting.

Ø Ø Ø

BALANCE

Even if we could live completely without sleep and other needs, we simply can't work on everything that interests us at once. One way I sometimes fail to take care of myself adequately is to work too much, not get enough sleep or food, etc.

We need to make choices to live more effectively, and practice enough self-respect and self-care to have the health and energy to pursue our passions.

Brian Tracy on the creative potential of balance

Liz Thompson of <u>Healthy Wealthy nWise Magazine</u> interviewed personal and business development coach and author Brian Tracy:

Liz: "Brian, you do so many different things. You ran for Governor, you're a speaker, you're an author, and you're a mentor. You've done hundreds of courses, written dozens of books… To the typical person, it would seem that you would have to go out of balance simply by focusing on all these different things at once. Has being out of balance ever stopped you or held you back from reaching your goals, have you ever been focused so much in one area that you became out of balance?"

Brian Tracy: "No, I don't get out of balance. I practice what I preach. In my book <u>Focal Point</u>, I explain how to develop a high level of effectiveness and simultaneously a high level of balance in every area of your life."

He says, "Once you get into it, it is very much like brushing your teeth every morning. You just simply get into a rhythm of living your life more and more effectively. The interesting thing is that everything is hard before it is easy."

Developing habits is always hard, he says, "but once you develop the habits, they are automatic and easy to follow and you get more and more effective at them. You get more and more done in less and less time as you develop these habits."

Positive habits

Tracy continues, "One of my big pushes in life is to help people develop excellent habits for themselves as their lives evolve so that those habits just lock in. Then they can concentrate on other things, but the habits of personal effectiveness, just simply go along like Old Man River.

"If you live in a monastery then maybe you don't have any problems. But since most of us don't, just look upon your life as a series of learning experiences. I love the idea that there is no such thing as failure, only feedback. Feedback just tells you that the particular direction that you are going in is not a great direction so you need to do something different."

From A Life on Fire – Living Your Life with Passion, Balance & Abundance – a free ebook collection of interviews with "some of the most successful, brilliant authors and speakers, with knowledge and inspiration for living a life of balanced abundance."

Also see more <u>Brian Tracy articles</u> and a variety of products at <u>Brian Tracy International</u>. Related site: <u>Your Success Store</u> - personal development programs, CDs, software, interviews from leaders like Robert Kiyosaki; Mark Victor Hansen; Jim Rohn; Denis Waitley; Connie Podesta, and others.

Ø Ø Ø

> *In conclusion*

MULTIPLE CHALLENGES - MULTIPLE REWARDS

One of the myths of highly talented people is they can choose whatever personal and career paths they want, and realize their abilities without hindrance. It doesn't necessarily work that inevitably, fluidly or easily. One way to better understand what challenges multitalented adults can face is to consider gifted kids.

In her Unwrapping the Gifted post "Multipotentiality," K-12 gifted education specialist Tamara Fisher quotes Bryant (a student-selected pseudonym), a graduating senior who lists his possible future careers as "applied psychologist, scientific psychologist, college teacher, philosophy, mathematics, architect, engineer."

He says, "I find it difficult to choose between careers because I fear how large the choice is. Having many options available is pleasant, but to determine what I will do for many years to come is scary."

Fisher notes, "Multipotentiality is the state of having many exceptional talents, any one or more of which could make for a great career for that person. She adds, "Gifted children often (though of course not always) have multipotentiality. Their advanced intellectual abilities and their intense curiosity make them prime candidates for excelling in multiple areas."

But, she adds, "This can be both a blessing and a curse. On the bright side, they have many realistic options for future careers. But on the downside, some of them will struggle mightily trying to decide which choice to make." She notes that having "so many great possible outcomes can be a source of debilitating stress."

That can be true for us as adults, too. Of course many people are able to realize multiple talents, and I have listed some examples in the Introduction and in other sections. But realizing multiple talents can be stressful and challenging in various ways, and that is something I have come to realize in living for decades past my high school and early college days when academic performance, at least, came fairly easily.

In her book "Smart Girls Two: A New Psychology of Girls, Women and Giftedness," Barbara Kerr (now a Distinguished Professor at The University of Kansas) makes comments about the drive for finding and realizing abilities that I really appreciate.

She writes, "I have observed in counseling talented adults that gifts seem to have their own insistence on acknowledgement. I never try to understand a musician separately from her music, or a scientist apart from her research, because if these outlets for talents are thwarted, the entire personality is threatened... Whenever a gift makes itself known - the the twelve year old who suddenly discovers the beauty and strength of her artwork, or the forty year old who at last gives way to her urge to create - that experience should be treated with respect, awe, and a sense of responsibility. It is the beginning of a heroic journey."

Underachieving - or just selective

Having advanced potential and exceptional capabilities in many talent areas also means, almost by definition, you are underachieving: you can't do everything.

One of the pleasures of my life has been pursuing serial interests in often radically different fields: being a research assistant in genetics and later in left/right brain wave research; a career counselor; a visual effects camera operator, and multiple other jobs and pursuits.

But among the 'costs' have been a life unmoored to any career path, often uncertain finances, and many periods of anxiety and self-doubt.

Thankfully, the series of sites I have created and keep developing is not only creatively rewarding, but also of value to other people.

In his article The Too Many Aptitudes Problem, Hank Pfeffer says, "Most people have about four or five strong talents... Most jobs require about four or five. As many as 10% of the population has double that number of aptitudes... There is evidence that people with too many aptitudes (TMAs) are less likely to obtain advanced education and/or succeed in a career than those with an average number of talents."

He notes, "Strong talents do not equal high performance. Having the right knacks or talents provides a head start and ongoing advantage. They are not very useful without knowledge and motivation."

He also points out, "Aptitudes have to be trained in order to be used well. Peak performance occurs when one has the right combination of talents, knowledge, motivation, opportunity, courage, luck, tools and the X factors."

And that also can mean every multitalented person may be "underachieving" when they do not have the adequate combination of internal, emotional and cognitive skills, plus endless and unpredictable external factors. In a very real sense, everyone may be called "underachieving" regardless of whether they are gifted or not.

One short definition is "Performance below potential."

But high ability and giftedness are much more than advanced potential, high scores and notable achievements. What really matters in talking about underachievement is the inner experience of "falling short of potential" – how that impacts our identity, esteem, life satisfaction and mental health.

Many of us are "naturally" self-critical, and not fulfilling more of the wide range of talents we have can be yet another source of fuel for calling ourselves deficient.

Read more in my post Adult underachievement – not living up to our high potential and see a video clip from a webinar presentation by SENG (Supporting Emotional Needs of the Gifted): "Understanding and Treating Anxiety, Depression, Bipolar Disorder and Underachievement in Gifted Children, Adolescents and Young Adults" – presented by Jerald Grobman, M.D.

Polyphrenia

Jean Houston [one of her books is A Passion for the Possible, among many others] commented in our interview about the quality of personal identity that can make us multifaceted: "Polyphrenia – the orchestration of our many selves – is our extended health. We have a vast crew within."

Houston thinks "a lot" of giftedness, though by no means all, "has to do with having a broader palette of perceptual capacity, being highly sensitive to all the senses, and also operating on different modes of intelligence" - not just the "standard brand" varieties of visual, kinesthetic and auditory, but also intuitive and emotional ones. She thinks, "When you have that, and you invest more time in it, you're just going to be taking in much more of your world; you're taking in a pluriverse all the time. And you're not living in an encapsulated state; you're available to the palette of the world, and thus available to many more patterns of possibility. And because your external sensibilities are so acute, your internal ones become equally so, and then that constellates as a pattern which is seen, touch, tasted, felt and emotionally juiced."

She also thinks the word "gifted" - like the word "psychic" rises and falls in popularity, and said, "Right now it's in a fallen state, and the thing is, you just find another set of metaphors." She suggests it could be a person saying "I'm someone who is really feeling my potential burgeoning within me, and I want to do something useful about it; I want to be of use to the world, and I'd like to use the best of what I have, to the degree that I can."

It can be very self-affirming to think of our complex inner life this way, with less concern for labels and external standards of giftedness, and with less self-critical concepts like "elitist" or "scattered" - though of course many people may have challenges such as adult ADHD.

J. Krishnamurti in his book <u>Think on These Things</u> declares, "Only the mind which has no walls, no foothold, no barrier, no resting place, which is moving completely with life, timelessly pushing on, exploring, exploding – only such a mind can be happy, eternally new, because it is creative in itself." (From my post <u>Being "scattered" and proud of it</u>.)

Creative polymathy

In his post "That's DR. Winnie to you: A New Child Star Stereotype" (on his Psychology Today blog), creativity researcher James C. Kaufman, Ph.D. writes about a number of people well-known as child stars, now grown, who have explored talents outside of acting. He writes: "One of the research topics in creativity that has always fascinated me has been creative polymathy – the ability to be creative in more than one domain."

One example he gives is Danica McKellar ('Winnie' on "The Wonder Years"), who earned her Ph.D. from UCLA in mathematics, and currently writes books promoting math. Another example being actor Mayim Bialik, who earned her Ph.D. from

UCLA in Neuroscience. On "The Big Bang Theory" TV series, she plays Amy Farrah Fowler, a neurobiologist and "not-girlfriend" of physicist Sheldon Cooper. Bialik has commented that "having an understanding of both mental illness and neurosis has been tremendously helpful to me in my acting career." See more in my post Developing multiple talents – the pleasures of creative polymathy.

~ ~

Thanks for reading. I hope this book has given you some helpful information and inspiration to better understand and make use of what Jean Houston called our "vast crew within" - our wealth of talents.

Ø Ø Ø

Notes about the author and book contents

Douglas Eby, M.A./Psychology, is a writer and researcher on the psychology of creative expression and personal growth, and author of the Talent Development Resources series of sites. He has been interested in these broad topics for most of his adult life, and has been writing and publishing articles for more than twenty years, including many interviews with actors, writers, directors and other artists, as well as with psychologists and creativity coaches.

Within the book are a number of quotations, which are used under Fair Use guidelines, with no intention to violate copyright.

For more material on enhancing creativity and personal growth, see the author's main site

<u>Talent Development Resources</u>
http://talentdevelop.com

Free PDF version

One of the values in this book is the large number of links to additional resources: websites, articles, books and more. Of course, these links are not visible or active in this paperback version - so as a bonus for purchasing the book, you can get a free PDF or ebook version.

Just use one of the following website addresses to get to a unique website page for book purchasers only, and sign up for the free Developing Talent newsletter, which provides weekly information and inspiration of the kind presented in this book. When you subscribe, you will immediately get a link to the PDF version of the book, and you may cancel the newsletter at any time.

Just enter one or the other of these URLs into your browser:

http://developingmultipletalents.com/guest/

http://bit.ly/DMT-PDF

Ø Ø Ø Ø

CPSIA information can be obtained
at www.ICGtesting.com
Printed in the USA
BVOW06s1514050118
504580BV00006B/22/P